Cryptography and Liberty 1999

An International Survey of Encryption Policy

Electronic Privacy Information Center
Washington, DC

About the Electronic Privacy Information Center

The Electronic Privacy Information Center (EPIC) is a public interest research center in Washington, D.C. It was established in 1994 to focus public attention on emerging civil liberties issues and to protect privacy, the First Amendment, and constitutional values. EPIC is a project of the Fund for Constitutional Government. EPIC works in association with Privacy International, an international human rights group based in London, UK and is also a member of the Global Internet Liberty Campaign, the Internet Free Expression Alliance and the Internet Privacy Coalition.

The EPIC Bookstore provides a comprehensive selection of books and reports on computer security, cryptography, the First Amendment and free speech, open government, and privacy. Visit the EPIC Bookstore at http://www.epic.org/bookstore/.

First edition 1999
Printed in the United States of America

ISBN: 1-893044-03-3

EPIC Staff

Marc Rotenberg, Executive Director

David L. Sobel, General Counsel

David Banisar, Policy Director

Shauna Van Dongen, Publications Director

Wayne Madsen, Senior Fellow

Acknowledgments

The Electronic Privacy Information Center gratefully acknowledges the support of the Open Society Institute, as well as the assistance of members of the EPIC Advisory Board and members of the Global Internet Liberty Campaign (GILC). The following individuals provided invaluable information and advice: Dr. Andrzej Adamski, Nicholas Copernicus University, Poland; Yaman Akdeniz, Cyber-Rights & Cyber-Liberties (UK); Michael Baker, EF Australia; Tracy Cohen, University of South Africa; Kenneth Neil Cukier, CommunicationsWeek International, France; Jos Dumortier, K.U.Leuven, Belgium; Rishab Aiyer Ghosh, India; Peter Gutmann, New Zealand; Austin Hill, ZKS, Canada; Prof. Masao Horibe, Chuo University, Japan; Bert-Jaap Koops, Tilburg University, NL; Meryem Marzouki, Imaginons un Réseau Internet Solidaire, France; Jose Luis Martin Mas, FREE, Spain; Viktor-Mayer-Schoenberger, Harvard University; Erich Moechel, quintessenz, Austria; Felipe Rodriquez, XS4ALL, NL; Per Helge Sørensen, Denmark; Greg Taylor, EF Australia; Peter Wallstrom; Sweden; Rigo Wenning, FITUG, Germany; Maurice Wessling, XS4ALL, NL.

Table of Contents

Executive Summary

Most countries in the world today have no controls on the use of cryptography. In the vast majority of countries, cryptography may be freely used, manufactured, and sold without restriction. This is true for both leading industrial countries and for developing countries. There is a movement towards international relaxation of regulations relating to encryption products, coupled with a rejection of key escrow and recovery policies. Many countries have recently adopted policies expressly rejecting requirements for key escrow systems and a few countries, most notably France, have dropped their escrow systems. There are a small number of countries where strong domestic controls on the use of cryptography exist. These are mostly countries where human rights command little respect.

Recent trends in international law and policy point toward continued relaxation of controls on cryptography. The Organization for Economic Cooperation and Development's Cryptography Policy Guidelines and the Ministerial Declaration of the European Union, both released in 1997, argue for the liberalization of controls on cryptography and the development of market-based, user driven cryptography products and services. There is a growing awareness worldwide of encryption and an increasing number of countries have developed policies, driven by the OECD guidelines.

Export controls remain the most powerful obstacle to the development and free flow of encryption. The revised December 1998 Wassenaar Arrangement may roll back some of the liberalization sought by the OECD, particularly by restricting the key lengths of encryption products that can be exported without approval licenses. However, several major countries have already indicated that they do not plan to adopt new restrictions.

The United States government continues to lead efforts for encryption controls around the world. The U.S. government has exerted economic and diplomatic pressure on other countries in an attempt to force them into adopting restrictive policies. The U.S. position may be explained, in part, by the dominant role that national intelligence and federal law enforcement agencies hold in the development of encryption policy.

The Importance of Cryptography

Emerging computer and communications technologies have radically altered the ways in which we communicate and exchange information. Along with the speed, efficiency, and cost-saving benefits of the digital revolution come new challenges to the security and privacy of communications and information traversing the global communications infrastructure.

In response to these challenges, the security mechanisms of traditional paper-based communications media -- envelopes and locked filing cabinets -- are being replaced by cryptographic security techniques. Through the use of cryptography, communication and information stored and transmitted by computers can be protected against interception to a very high degree. Until recently, there was little non-governmental demand for encryption capabilities. Modern encryption technology -- a mathematical process involving the use of formulas (or algorithms) -- was traditionally deployed most widely to protect the confidentiality of military and diplomatic communications. With the advent of the computer revolution and recent innovations in the science of encryption, a new market for cryptographic products has developed. Electronic communications are now widely used in the civilian sector and have become an integral component of the global economy. Computers store and exchange an ever-increasing amount of highly personal information, including medical and financial data. In this electronic environment, the need for privacy-enhancing technologies is apparent. Communications applications such as electronic mail and electronic fund transfers require secure means of encryption and authentication -- features that can only be provided if cryptographic know-how is widely available and unencumbered by government regulation.

Cryptography can also be used to allow for the anonymous dissemination of information, such as reports on human rights abuses, and to ensure that documents of human rights groups are not tampered with or altered after release.

Governmental regulation of cryptographic security techniques endangers personal privacy. Encryption ensures the confidentiality of personal records, such as medical information, personal financial data, and electronic mail. In a networked environment, such information is increasingly at risk of being stolen or misused.

Encryption and Human Rights

Government regulation of techniques such as encryption that help to protect individual privacy may also be contrary to the spirit of international laws and norms that recognize privacy as a fundamental human right. Article 12 of the Universal Declaration of Human Rights, Article 17 of the International Covenant on Civil and Political Rights, as well as other international agreements, and national laws, make clear the importance of privacy protection for human freedom and civil society.

In many countries in the world, human rights organizations, journalists and political dissidents are the most common targets of surveillance by government intelligence and law enforcement agencies and other non-governmental groups. The U.S. Department of State, in its 1996 *Country Reports on Human Rights Practices*, reported widespread illegal or uncontrolled use of wiretaps by both government and private groups in over 90 countries. In some countries, such as Honduras and Paraguay, the state-owned telecommunications companies were active participants in helping the security services monitor human rights advocates. These problems are not limited to developing countries. French counter-intelligence agents wiretapped the telephones of prominent journalists and opposition party leaders. The French Commission Nationale de Contrôle des Interceptions de Securité estimated that there are some 100,000 illegal taps conducted each year in France. There have been numerous cases in the United Kingdom which revealed that the British intelligence services monitor social activists, labor unions and civil liberties organizations. A recent UK bill was enacted that allows for the surveillance of lawyers and priests. In Germany, a bill is currently pending that would allow, for the first time since the Nazi era, the ability to bug journalists' offices. The European Parliament issued a report in January 1998 revealing that the U.S. National Security Agency was conducting massive monitoring of European communications.

Many human rights groups currently use encryption to protect their files and communications from seizure and interception by the governments they monitor for abuses. These include Guatemala, Ethiopia, Haiti, Mexico, South

Africa, Hong Kong and Turkey. Other groups such as Amnesty International USA also use cryptographic techniques to digitally sign messages that they send over the Internet to ensure that the messages are not altered in transmission.

Additional information on the use of encryption technology by international human rights organizations is contained in the briefing paper "Encryption in the Service of Human Rights," produced by Human Rights Watch (http://www.aaas.org/SPP/DSPP/CSTC/ briefings/crypto/dinah.htm)

GILC and Encryption

The Global Internet Liberty Campaign (GILC) was established in June 1996 to protect civil liberties and human rights in the online world. GILC maintains a web site, publishes an on-line newsletter, and participates in government meetings around the globe. GILC is made up of over 50 human rights, consumer, privacy, free speech, and Internet user groups in 20 countries on five continents.

GILC has been active in promoting the worldwide elimination of restrictions on encryption. GILC members have made presentations to the OECD, the EU and other international organizations, organized policy conferences in many countries, and submitted comments and reports to international governmental groups and governments. Members of GILC provide training in the use of cryptographic methods to human rights organizers, journalists and political activists.

In 1996, GILC issued a "Resolution in Support of the Freedom to Use Cryptography" that states: "the use of cryptography implicates human rights and matters of personal liberty that affect individuals around the world" and that "the privacy of communication is explicitly protected by Article 12 of the Universal Declaration of Human Rights, Article 17 of the International Covenant on Civil and Political Rights, and national law." [1]

GILC also maintains an extensive collection of resources about encryption policy on its web site at (http://www.gilc.org/).

---

[1] See Resolution in Support of the Freedom to Use Cryptography, September 25, 1996 (Appendix C).

Purpose and Methodology of the Survey

This survey was undertaken by the Electronic Privacy Information Center (EPIC), with the assistance of members of the Global Internet Liberty Campign and other experts on encryption policy, to provide a comprehensive review of the cryptography policies of virtually every national and territorial jurisdiction in the world.

To obtain information for the survey, we sent letters to the embassies, United Nations missions, government ministries, trade boards, and information offices of some 230 countries and territories with independent policy-making authority. These entities were contacted in the belief that governments themselves are best able to authoritatively explain their policies, especially on such a technical subject. We patterned our survey after one conducted in 1989 by the Computer Science and Law Research Group (GRID) of the University of Quebec, which analyzed the data protection policies and laws of over 150 countries on behalf of the government of Canada. In this second survey, we expanded the contacts to include organizations and individuals in various countries with direct knowledge of encryption and telecommunications policies. We inquired about four major areas of cryptography policy:

- controls maintained by the governments on the domestic use of cryptography in their countries;
- controls maintained by the governments on the importation to their countries of computer programs or equipment that permit cryptography;
- controls maintained by the governments on the exportation of domestically developed computer programs or equipment that permit cryptography; and
- identification of the agency or department of the governments responsible for setting policy on the use, importation, or exportation of cryptographic technology.

Between the issuance of our first report in February 1998 and this one, the Organization of Economic Cooperation and Development (OECD) conducted an inventory of cryptography regulations of its member states. We have incorporated those findings in this report as they best represent current national policies within the OECD member countries.

We also referred to a report prepared by the U.S. Department of Commerce and the National Security Agency for the Interagency Working Group on Encryption and Telecommunications Policy, obtained by EPIC under the Freedom of Information Act. The report, dated July 1995, is titled "A Study of the International Market for Computer Software with Encryption". The Commerce Department and NSA attempted to obtain and analyze copies of the laws and regulations from as many encryption-producing nations as possible.

In this and the previous survey, we consulted the very useful Crypto Law Survey that is maintained by Bert-Jaap Koops. That survey includes descriptions of crypto policies in many of the world's countries as well as links to important source documents. [2]

A 100 per cent response was the goal of this and our previous survey. For this survey we found that many more countries were familiar with the issue than had been during the first survey.

Country Ratings

Reported countries have been grouped into three categories regarding controls on cryptography. A "Green" designation signifies that the country promotes or has expressed support for a policy that allows for unhindered legal use of cryptography, such as adopting the OECD Guidelines. A "Yellow" designation signifies that the country has proposed new domestic cryptography controls, including domestic use controls, has import controls, or has shown a willingness to abide strictly by the terms of the Wassenaar Arrangement. A "Red" designation denotes countries that have instituted sweeping controls on cryptography, including domestic use controls. Many countries do not fit neatly into one of the three categories, but may share attributes from two of the categories. These countries are designated as "Green/Yellow" or "Yellow/Red."

Survey Results

Few Domestic Controls

Most countries do not restrict the domestic use of encryption by their citizens. Of the handful of countries around the world that do, few are democracies and most have strong authoritarian governments. The countries include Belarus, China, Israel, Kazakhstan, Pakistan, Russia, Singapore, Tunisia, Vietnam, and Venezuela. In many of those countries, the controls do not appear to be enforced.

Most countries that have explicitly rejected controls have noted the importance of security of electronic information for electronic commerce, the threats of economic espionage, and the need to protect privacy online. The 1997 OECD Guidelines on Cryptography Policy and the European Commission expressed strong support for the unrestricted development of encryption products and services. In the past year, Canada, Ireland, and Finland have announced national crypto policies based on the OECD Guidelines, favoring the free use of encryption

A number of countries explicitly reversed their positions on domestic controls recently. Most notable of these is France, which has long restricted encryption, but reversed that policy in January 1999 and announced that people will be able to use encryption without restrictions. In December 1997, Belgium amended its 1994 law to eliminate its provision restricting cryptography.

Little Support for Key Escrow/Key Recovery

Concurrent with the rejection of domestic controls by most countries is the rejection of key escrow/recovery policies by governments. We found that few countries now support such policies.

---

[2] See <http://cwis.kub.nl/~frw/people/koops/lawsurvy.htm>.

Key escrow/recovery was a concept promoted by the United States government whereby users would be able to use strong encryption in their systems. However, a third party such as a government agency or a specially authorized company (which usually had government ties) would hold the keys and provide them to a government agency when requested. Escrow was first introduced in the U.S. in the Clipper Chip in 1993. Security experts have been critical of the security of escrow systems, noting a number of problems created by having a central party holding users' keys.

The U.S. pressured many countries and international organizations such as the OECD and Wassenaar to adopt key escrow. U.S. Envoy for Encryption David Aaron traveled the world urging countries to adopt escrow policies. The OECD countries rejected the U.S. pressure and called for free use of cryptography and respect for privacy.

A critical and perhaps final blow to key escrow was the rejection of key escrow by the Wassenaar Arrangement group in 1998. The U.S. attempted to gain favorable export rules for escrow/recovery products to encourage an international market. No consensus was reached and this plan was rejected. The German Ministry of Economics announced in a press release: "Certain states that had originally demanded special treatment for key recovery products were unsuccessful in their efforts. The export of encryption technology will therefore remain possible without the deposit of keys with the government."

These international policy developments have had a significant impact on domestic policies in both countries that supported escrow and those that did not have encryption policies. The most dramatic turnaround was in France, where Prime Minister Jospin announced in January 1999 that France would scrap its key escrow system in favor of free use of cryptography. Taiwan, which had stated in 1997 that it was planning a key escrow system, is now reporting that it does not plan to adopt a key escrow system.

Only a few countries now officially endorse key escrow. Spain enacted a telecommunications bill in 1998 that may promote escrow, but it has not been implemented. The UK was in the process of developing an electronic commerce bill that may coerce Certificate Authorities to obtain private keys as a condition of licensing and new laws that will require disclosure of keys by users. However, that effort now appears to have lost support and may be withdrawn. In the U.S., export control rules that once encouraged key escrow were somewhat relaxed in 1998. Lacking any real international consensus, it appears unlikely that escrow will survive.

Increase in Surveillance Budgets and Powers

As countries reject restrictions on encryption, they continue to face pressure from law enforcement and intelligence agencies which demand access to communications. There have been a variety of approached taken to resolve this pressure.

One trend has been the increased funding of intelligence agencies to compensate for the perceived loss of intelligence from encryption. In the United States, a number of new "Net Centers" have been proposed. These Net Centers would combine government and private sector money and would not be subject to freedom of information laws.[3] In France, Prime Minister Jospin announced that as part of France's relaxation of controls, "the technical capacities of the authorities will be significantly reinforced." In Australia, a government report recommended that agencies be given additional powers to "hack" into computer systems under a court order. In Germany, police are now allowed to place microphones in homes. The Council of Europe is also developing a new Convention on Computer Crime that will reportedly encourage new surveillance powers and centers at the urging of the U.S. Department of Justice, which is drafting the convention. These new proposals for new investigative powers raise troubling questions about surveillance and accountability. Will the agencies granted these powers be fully accountable to democratic institutions and subject to meaningful public oversight?

Other countries such as Malaysia and Ireland are enacting laws that require individuals to hand over keys for criminal investigations. Such approaches raise issues involving the right against self-incrimination, which is respected in many countries worldwide.

The Role of Export Controls

[3] http://www.epic.org/security/infowar/epic-cip.html

Internationally, export controls are the strongest tool used by governments to limit development of encryption products. Export controls reduce the availability of encryption in common programs such as operating systems, electronic mail and word processors, especially from American companies. The restrictions make it difficult to develop international standards for encryption and interoperability of different programs. Countries must develop their own local programs, which do not inter-operate well (if at all) with other programs developed independently in other countries. They may not be as secure because of a lack of peer-review. Because markets are smaller, companies and individuals are not as interested in developing programs because of smaller potential profits.

Some countries have taken advantage of the situation by promoting the lack of controls in their countries. As Switzerland noted in response to our inquiry, "Switzerland will keep its efficient export permit process for cryptographic goods in order to encourage Swiss exports to increase their sales and share worldwide while being mindful of national security interests." One result of this has been the emergence of small companies in many countries without restrictions, which produce encryption products. Another result has been companies, especially American companies, moving their encryption production divisions overseas to countries with fewer controls, such as Switzerland.

The Internet has significantly changed the effectiveness of export controls. Strong, unbreakable encryption programs can now be delivered in seconds to anywhere in the world from anywhere with a network connection. It has been increasingly difficult for countries to limit dissemination, and once a program is released, it is nearly impossible to stop its redissemination, especially if it is in one of the many countries around the world with no export controls. In the United States, export controls are used as a justification to limit of the availability of encryption on domestic Internet sites and thus serve as indirect domestic controls on encryption.

The Wassenaar Arrangement

The Wassenaar Arrangement (WA) is an agreement by a group of 33 industrialized countries to restrict the export of conventional weapons and "dual use" technology to certain other countries considered pariah states or, in some cases, those that are at war. Certain cryptographic products, along with other technology such as supercomputers and high-level computer security access software, are considered to be "dual use" in that they can be used for both commercial and military purposes. The WA replaces the former Cold War-era Coordinating Committee on Multilateral Export Controls (COCOM), a group of 17 countries that placed restrictions on the export of certain technology to countries of the former Warsaw Pact and other communist states. After the fall of the Warsaw Pact and Soviet Union, COCOM became an anachronism, and on November 16, 1993, in The Hague, COCOM agreed to dissolve itself and to establish a grouping called the "New Forum."

At a New Forum meeting held in Wassenaar, the Netherlands, it was decided that COCOM would formally cease to exist on March 31, 1994. The New Forum agreed to continue the use of the COCOM munitions control lists as a basis for global export controls until the new arrangement could be established. A formal agreement to establish the "Wassenaar Arrangement" was reached at the December 19, 1995, meeting in Wassenaar. The participating countries agreed to locate the Wassenaar Arrangement Secretariat in Vienna. The WA is one of four international export control arrangements. The others are the Nuclear Suppliers Group, the Australia Group, and the Missile Technology Control Regime and are mainly directed against the proliferation of weapons of mass destruction and missiles.

The WA is open on a global basis to other countries that comply with the export control criteria. To be admitted to the Arrangement, a country must: 1) be a producer and/or exporter of arms or dual-use industrial equipment; 2) maintain non-proliferation policies and appropriate national policies, including adherence to international non-proliferation regimes and treaties; and 3) maintain fully effective export controls. Although the Arrangement does not provide for observer status, an outreach policy is being planned to inform non-member countries about WA objectives and activities and encourage such non-members to adopt WA-compliant national policies on the export of conventional arms and dual-use technologies, including cryptography.

The Unclear Authority of Wassenaar

It is important to note that the WA is neither an international treaty nor a law. It is merely designed to exchange views and information on international trade in conventional arms and dual-use goods and technologies. Also, Participating States commit to adjust their national export control policies to adhere to the WA Control Lists, but this commitment is discretionary in nature and not mandatory. Participating States may adjust their cryptographic export policies through new regulations or legislation.

The WA representatives largely represent the law enforcement, signals intelligence, and weapons control sectors of participant governments and have little appreciation for commercial concerns. The WA maintains that it is not directed at impeding bona fide commerce and is not directed against any state or group of states. However, the list of countries covered by a participating state's own national sanctions varies widely. For example, the United States imposes sanctions on certain countries through the International Traffic in Arms Regulations and the Export Administration Regulations, which are supervised by the Departments of Commerce, Treasury, and State.[4] The United Kingdom also imposes sanctions on countries, but its list differs from that of the United States.[5] Russia maintains virtually no enforceable sanctions on other countries. The substantial differences between participants on sanctions are an important weakness in the application of uniform WA export controls.

The WA countries maintain export controls for the items on the agreed control lists, which are reviewed periodically to take into account technological developments and experience gained. One such review took place throughout 1998 and resulted in a change to the cryptography dual-use control list. The WA announced the revised list on December 3, 1998. Decisions to amend the Control Lists, as with all WA decisions, are made by consensus, i.e., they must be unanimous.

---

[4] Countries to which the United States imposes sanctions are: Cuba, Iran, Iraq, Libya, North Korea, and the Angolan opposition group UNITA (National Union for the Total Independence of Angola) and UNITA-controlled area of Angola. In addition, certain entities in China, India, Israel, Pakistan, and Wassenaar partner Russia are subject to special export determination for some technologies, including cryptography.

[5] The United Kingdom maintains sanctions against Iran, Iraq, Libya, Myanmar (Burma), Nigeria, Taiwan, and Yugoslavia. Unlike the United States, the British maintain sanctions against Argentina, a Wassenaar partner but not against Cuba, which is subject to an American embargo. Portugal, a Wassenaar partner, maintains sanctions against Indonesia, which is not subject to American or British sanctions. On April 10, 1998, several WA partners of the United States abstained in a UN Human Rights Commission condemning economic sanctions as coercive. They included Austria, the Czech Republic, Denmark, Ireland, Italy, Poland and the Ukraine.

The WA also facilitates the sharing of export information between participating states. Countries are required to report transfers or denials of transfers of certain controlled dual-use items to the other WA participants. Of particular interest to WA members are denials for export licenses for sensitive technology. Therefore, the WA stipulates that members will agree that notification of other members shall be made on an early and timely basis, preferably within 30 days but no later than within 60 days of the date of the denial of the license.

The New Wassenaar List of Dual-Use Goods and Technologies

On December 3, 1998 the Wassenaar Secretariat announced that new cryptography guidelines had been added to the Arrangement. The Wassenaar Dual-Use Control List now extends to encryption hardware and software cryptography products above 56-bits. These include Web browsers, e-mail applications, electronic commerce servers, and telephone scrambling devices. Other mass-market products, such as personal computer operating systems, word processing, and data base programs having strengths over 64-bits are subject to controls for two years. These controls must be renewed and approved unanimously, otherwise they will be canceled. There remains confusion over the control list's distinction between 56 and 64-bit encryption, but it appears that participating states are obligated to establish new export controls over "mass market" encryption software that uses keys longer than 64-bits. They must also restrict other symmetric encryption software and hardware having keys longer than 56-bits (unless a formal export license is issued by the respective national government).

The Wassenaar countries also agreed to control other software, such as that used in specific sectors such as banking, insurance and health, at the 56-bit level. According to a press release from the German Ministry of Economy, "Certain states that had initially demanded special treatment for 'key recovery' products have not been successful. These were seen to be the United States and United Kingdom. Thus, the export of encryption technology will remain possible without depositing keys with government agencies." The restrictions do not apply to encryption products that protect intellectual property, such as digital watermarking for items like videos, cassettes and DVD disks. This exemption is seen as a concession to the entertainment industry.

Most importantly, and in what constitutes an important loophole, the new WA controls do not apply to the “intangible” distribution of cryptography, including downloads from the Internet.

It remains to be seen what the effects will actually be on the flow of encryption products. Several countries such as Canada and Germany have indicated that they do not plan to impose new strict restrictions on exports of mass-market software. The Swiss government wrote that "the upcoming minor changes to Switzerland's export controls on cryptographic goods as a result of the December changes to Wassenaar will not alter the liberal Swiss Cryptography Policy."

The International Development of Encryption Policy

Over the past several years, the role of international organizations has become crucial in the development of encryption policies. These fora include the Organization for Economic Cooperation and Development, the European Union, the G-7/G-8, the Council of Europe, and the Wassenaar Arrangement (see above). In all of these, the U.S. -- with the support of the UK Government -- has led efforts to gain international support for restrictions. The U.S. have been led by the Undersecretary of Commerce for International Trade and former Ambassador to the OECD, David Aaron, who traveled the world urging governments to support the U.S. positions. In certain fora, especially in those which are oriented towards law enforcement or military/intelligence issues, the U.S. has had some success. Opposition to these efforts often has been led by Germany and the Scandinavian countries.

Organization for Economic Cooperation and Development

The Organization for Economic Cooperation and Development (OECD) is a Paris-based international body of 29 countries.

In 1996, the U.S. government approached the OECD to recommend that it begin work on cryptography guidelines focusing on international compatibility. The OECD had previously developed well respected guidelines on the privacy of personal information and computer security. The U.S. began pressuring the OECD to adopt key escrow as an international standard. For its encryption deliberations, the OECD changed from its traditional two year process of consensus to a one year accelerated process with a "core group" writing the guidelines. At the meetings, the U.S. delegation, led by the Justice Department, the FBI, and the NSA, lobbied the committee to endorse key escrow.

The OECD was severely divided by the proposals. The U.S. position was supported by France and the United Kingdom. On the other side, the Japanese Ministry of Trade and Industry was strongly opposed. The Scandinavian countries also announced that they were unhappy with the proposals, stating that the system would undermine trust. Denmark's representative announced that key escrow would not be included in a nation-wide card system. Industry representatives wanted to ensure that they would have the right to adopt any system of their choosing.

In March 1997, the OECD issued its Guidelines on Cryptography Policy. The OECD recommendation is a non-binding agreement that identifies the basic issues that countries should consider in establishing cryptography policies at the national and international level.

The OECD Cryptography Guidelines state:

> The need for Guidelines emerged from the explosive worldwide growth of information and communications networks and technologies and the requirement for effective protection of the data which is transmitted and stored on those systems. Cryptography is a fundamental tool in a comprehensive data security system. Cryptography can also ensure confidentiality and integrity of data and provide mechanisms for authentication and non-repudiation for use in electronic commerce.
>
> Governments want to encourage the use of cryptography for its data protection benefits and commercial applications, but they are challenged to draft cryptography policies which balance the various interest at stake, including privacy, law enforcement, national

security, technology development and commerce. International consultation and co-operation must drive cryptography policy because of the inherently international nature of information and communications networks and the difficulties of defining and enforcing jurisdictional boundaries in the new global environment."

The Guidelines are intended to promote the use of cryptography, to develop electronic commerce through a variety of commercial applications, to bolster user confidence in networks, and to provide for data security and privacy protection.

Some OECD Member countries have already implemented policies and laws on cryptography, and many countries are still developing them. Failure to co-ordinate these national policies at the international level could introduce obstacles to the evolution of national and global information and communications networks and could impede international trade. OECD governments have recognized the importance of international co-operation, and the OECD has contributed by developing consensus on specific policy and regulatory issues related to cryptography and, more broadly, to information and communications networks and technologies.

The Guidelines set out eight basic Principles for cryptography policy:

1. Cryptographic methods should be trustworthy in order to generate confidence in the use of information and communications systems.

2. Users should have a right to choose any cryptographic method, subject to applicable law.

3. Cryptographic methods should be developed in response to the needs, demands and responsibilities of individuals, businesses and governments.

4. Technical standards, criteria and protocols for cryptographic methods should be developed and promulgated at the national and international level.

5. The fundamental rights of individuals to privacy, including secrecy of communications and protection of personal data, should be respected in national cryptography policies and in the implementation and use of cryptographic methods.

6. National cryptography policies may allow lawful access to plaintext, or cryptographic keys, of encrypted data. These policies must respect the other principles contained in the guidelines to the greatest extent possible.

7. Whether established by contract or legislation, the liability of individuals and entities that offer cryptographic services or hold or access cryptographic keys should be clearly stated.

8. Governments should co-operate to co-ordinate cryptography policies. As part of this effort, governments should remove, or avoid creating in the name of cryptography policy, unjustified obstacles to trade.

The OECD is currently planning to conduct a follow up to the guidelines in the area of digital signatures. In October 1998, the OECD released a survey of the member countries which found that many have adopted the guidelines.

The European Union

The European Union has played a key role in rejecting restrictions on encryption. The European Commission requires Member States to report to the Commission any national proposals to impose technical rules for marketing, use, manufacture, or import of cryptographic products. The Commission also seeks to dismantle intra-Union controls on commercial encryption products.

In October 1997, the European Commission's Directorate-General XIII, which is responsible for Telecommunications, Information Market and Exploitation of Research, issued a report that took issue with the United States' policy of encouraging key escrow and recovery schemes. The report stated that "restricting the use of encryption could well prevent law-abiding companies and citizens from protecting themselves against criminal attacks," adding that key escrow systems "would not . . . totally prevent criminals from using these technologies."[6]

On the issue of "back door" mechanisms giving law enforcement and intelligence agencies the right to read the plaintext of encrypted messages, the report said that if such systems are required, they "should be limited to what is absolutely necessary."

The report was sent by the European Commission to the major bodies of the European Union, including the European Parliament, the Council of Ministers, the Economic and Social Committee and the Committee of the Regions.

However, a European Council Resolution of January 17, 1995, requires network operators and service providers to provide law enforcement agencies "in the clear" access to encrypted communications.

In 1992, the European Commission proposed a dual-use regulation as part of the progression to the free market. Since military exports were linked to Member States' national security concerns, control of such exports was deemed to be a matter for individual states. However, with dual-use goods, it was argued that, while military uses were of a national interest, their civil use was in the purview of the European Commission.

Eventually, a compromise was reached. A dual-use Regulation was agreed upon. The basis for the regulation was Article 113 of the Treaty of Rome and a Maastricht-based Common Foreign and Security Policy Joint Action with a series of annexes. The EU's dual-use Regulation (EC No. 3381/94) contains 24 articles and it entered into force on July 1, 1995. Council Decision No. 94/942/CFSP, with 8 articles and 5 annexes, has been appended to it.

The series of regulations, decisions, and annexes state that:

- all Member States recognize the same list of dual-use goods (generally based on the COCOM and Wassenaar lists), destinations, and guidelines;

---

6 EU Communication on Digital Signatures and Encryption (97)503 <http//www.ispo.cec.be/eif/policy>

- the majority of dual-use goods may require, at most, only a general authorization license for shipment between member states (and for favored destinations outside the Union; Australia, Canada, Japan, Norway, Switzerland, and the United States). This amounts to EU domestic controls on products shipped between Member States;
- a common level of export control should exist throughout the Union; and
- an export license issued in one Member State shall normally be valid for the shipment of goods from another Member State.

On May 15, 1998, the Commission adopted a Proposal for a Council Regulation setting up an EU regime for the control of exports of dual-use goods and technology (COM(1998) 257 final, 98/0162 (ACC)). The proposal calls for a notification procedure for intra-Community transfers of cryptographic products instead of the current authorization/licensing scheme.

G-8

The Group of 8 (G-8) is made up of the heads of state of the top eight industrialized countries in the world. The leaders have been meeting annually since 1975 to discuss issues of importance, including the information highway, crime and terrorism.

The G8 has been active in discussing encryption policy at the urging of the United States. At the G8 meeting in Lyon, France in 1996, the G8 agreed to "accelerate consultations, in appropriate bilateral or multilateral fora, on the use of encryption that allows, when necessary, lawful government access to data and communications in order to, inter alia, prevent or investigate acts of terrorism, while protecting the privacy of legitimate communications." [7]

At the Denver Summit in June 1997, the G8 agreed: "To counter, inter alia, the use of strong encryption by terrorists, we have endorsed acceleration of consultations and adoption of the OECD guidelines for cryptography policy and invited all states to develop national policies on encryption, including key, management, which may allow, consistent with these guidelines. lawful

---

[7] Ministerial Conference on Terrorism, Paris, France, July 30, 1996, Agreement on 25 Measures. <http://utl1.library.utoronto.ca/disk1/www/documents/g7/terror25.htm>

government access to prevent and investigate acts of terrorism and to find a mechanism to cooperate internationally in implementing such policies. "

At the Birmingham, England meeting on May 18, 1998, the G8 adopted a recommendation on ten principles and a ten-point action on high-tech crime that did not explicitly mention encryption. The ministers announced, "We call for close cooperation with industry to reach agreement on a legal framework for obtaining, presenting and preserving electronic data as evidence, while maintaining appropriate privacy protection, and agreements on sharing evidence of those crimes with international partners. This will help us combat a wide range of crime, including abuse of the Internet and other new technologies."[8]

The next G8 meeting will be in Cologne, Germany on June 18-20, 1999.

Council of Europe

The Council of Europe is an inter-governmental organization formed in 1949 by West European countries. There are now 40 member countries.[9] Its main role is "to strengthen democracy, human rights and the rule of law throughout its member states." Its description also notes that "it acts as a forum for examining a whole range of social problems, such as social exclusion, intolerance, the integration of migrants, the threat to private life posed by new technology, bioethical issues, terrorism, drug trafficking and criminal activities."

On September 8, 1995, the Council of Europe approved a recommendation to limit strong cryptography in their member states. The Council is not like the European Commission in that it has no statutory authority to enforce its recommendations. However it is rare for member countries to reject Council of Europe's recommendations. The Recommendation of the Committee of

---

8 G-8 Communique, Birmingham, England, May 18, 1998 <http://www.gilc.org/crypto/g7/g8-birmingham-598.html>

9 http://www.coe.fr/eng/std/states.htm

Ministers to Member States Concerning Problems of Criminal Procedure Law Connected with Information[10] states:

> "Subject to legal privileges or protection, investigating authorities should have the power to order persons who have data in a computer system under their control to provide all necessary information to enable access to a computer system and the data therein. Criminal procedure law should ensure that a similar order can be given to other persons who have knowledge about the functioning of the computer system or measures applied to secure the data therein."

> "Specific obligations should be imposed on operators of public and private networks that offer telecommunications services to the public to avail themselves of all necessary technical measures that enable the interception of telecommunications by the investigating authorities."

> "Specific obligations should be imposed on service providers who offer telecommunications services to the public, either through public or private networks, to provide information to identify the user, when so ordered by the competent investigating authority."

> "Measures should be considered to minimize the negative effects of the use of cryptography on the investigation of criminal offenses, without affecting its legitimate use more than is strictly necessary."

The Council is now working on a draft directive on computer crime. This directive is being drafted in part by the Computer Crime Division of the U.S. Department of Justice, which unsuccessfully represented the U.S. at the OECD. The drafts reportedly call for increased surveillance powers.

---

10 Recommendation No. R (95) 13 of the Committee of Ministers to Member States Concerning Problems of Criminal Procedure Law Connected with Information Technology (Adopted by the Committee of Ministers on 11 September 1995) <http://www.privacy.org/pi/intl_orgs/coe/info_tech_1995.html>

Country Reports

Angola

1999 UNKNOWN
1998 Not reported

According to the Angolan Embassy in Washington, D.C., the Ministry of Science and Technology in Luanda is responsible for setting cryptographic policy. A fax sent to that agency went unanswered.

Ref: Embassy of Angola fax dated January 19, 1999.

Anguilla

1999 GREEN
1998 GREEN

Anguilla is a self-governing British territory in the Caribbean. It has also attracted an off-shore Internet industry that takes advantage of the territory's tax haven status. It has no restrictions on cryptography.

Offshore Information Services is one company that offers Anguilla domain name services (.ai), e-mail accounts, virtual web sites, and links to encryption programs like Pretty Good Privacy (PGP). It also offers the opportunity to engage in cryptographic civil disobedience. One may send a three-line encryption program to Anguilla. In the United States, this simple harmless act is illegal, and a violation of the U.S. export control rules. The web address for the civil disobedience campaign is http://online.offshore.com.ai/arms-trafficker/.

On September 16, 1998, the United States authorized the export of unlimited strength encryption products (with or without key recovery) to the banking and financial, insurance, health and medical, and on-line electronic commercial sectors in Anguilla. This is an indication that the U.S. has leveraged its authority to gain access to plain text information in those sectors within the country under Mutual Legal Assistance Treaty (MLAT)/Financial Action Task Force (FATF) provisions.

Ref: Charles Platt, "Plotting Away in Margaritaville," *Wired* (July 1997)
White House Press Release, September 16, 1998.

Antigua and Barbuda

1999 GREEN
1998 GREEN

The Embassy of Antigua and Barbuda in Washington did not respond to our survey. However, a review of their Free Trade Zone web site yielded the fact that the island nation is trying to compete with Anguilla in luring international data services, including those reliant on the Internet. Several virtual casinos have been established in the Free Trade Zone. It is certain that strong encryption is a high priority for such operations.

On September 16, 1998, the United States authorized the export of unlimited strength encryption products (with or without key recovery) to the banking and financial, insurance, health and medical, and on-line electronic commercial sectors in Antigua and Barbuda. This is an indication that the U.S. has leveraged its authority to gain access to plain text information in those sectors within the country under Mutual Legal Assistance Treaty (MLAT)/Financial Action Task Force (FATF) provisions.

Ref: www.candw.ag/~ftpzone/gam elicenced.htm
White House Press Release, September 16, 1998.

Argentina

1999 GREEN/YELLOW
1998 YELLOW

Argentina imposes no import or domestic use controls on cryptography.

The Secretariat for Public Affairs manages the Public Key Infrastructure for the Federal Government Administration, and as such, has issued Technical Standards related to the use of public key certificates for government bodies.

Argentina has acceded to the Wassenaar Arrangement and is committed to restricting the export of cryptographic products and technology as dual-use goods, including the new controls announced in December 1998.

On September 16, 1998, the United States authorized the export of unlimited strength encryption products (with or without key recovery) to the banking and financial, insurance, health and medical, and on-line electronic commercial sectors in Argentina. This is an indication that the U.S. has leveraged its authority to gain access to plain text information in those sectors within the country under Mutual Legal Assistance Treaty (MLAT)/Financial Action Task Force (FATF) provisions.

Ref: Email communication from the Secretariat for Public Affairs, January 1999.
White House Press Release, September 16, 1998.

Armenia

1999 GREEN/YELLOW
1998 YELLOW

According to the Second Secretary of the Embassy of Armenia in Washington, Armenia does not currently have a policy on the use of cryptography. However, the Armenian government has recently set up a Department of Information and Publications which, among other things, is planning to initiate legislation concerning the use of cryptography.

Ref: Embassy of the Republic of Armenia letter dated July 31, 1997.

Aruba

1999 GREEN
1998 Not reported

There are no domestic controls on the use of encryption.

On September 16, 1998, the United States authorized the export of unlimited strength encryption products (with or without key recovery) to the banking and financial, insurance, health and medical, and on-line electronic commercial sectors in Aruba. This is an indication that the U.S. has leveraged its authority to gain access to plain text information in those sectors within the country under Mutual Legal Assistance Treaty (MLAT)/Financial Action Task Force (FATF) provisions.

Ref: White House Press Release, September 16, 1998.

Australia

1999 GREEN/YELLOW
1998 GREEN/YELLOW

During our first survey we received a phone call from the Embassy of Australia in Washington, D.C. They said they had received our request for information on Australia's laws on the use, export, and import of cryptographic products but were unsure to which agency of the Australian government to forward our request. The confusion by the embassy on which government department is responsible for cryptography was cited in the government-commissioned "*Review of Policy relating to Encryption Technologies*", authored by former deputy director of the Australia Security Intelligence Organization (ASIO), Gerard Walsh. In what is popularly called the Walsh Report (issued on October 10, 1996 and embargoed by the government for public release until a Freedom of Information Act request by Electronic Frontiers Australia), Walsh criticized the government for its lack of coordination in establishing a cryptographic policy. In addition, the Review found a lack of clarity as to which Minister and which department had responsibility for cryptography policy and the consequent danger of a lack of coordination in policy development.

For this survey, we received feedback directly from the Attorney General's Department and the Defense Signals Directorate (DSD) of Australia. The DSD and AG letters state:

1. There are no restrictions on the use of cryptographic software and hardware within Australia.
2. There are no controls on the import of cryptography software and hardware into Australia.
3. There are controls on the export of cryptographic software and hardware. There are no separate controls for non-tangible exports. Australia will continue to implement export controls consistent with our international responsibilities under the Wassenaar Arrangement.
4. Cryptographic policy (with the exception of export controls) is the responsibility of the Attorney General's Department. Export controls of cryptographic software and hardware is administered by the Department of Defense and enforced by the Australian Customs Service.

Despite earlier expectations, the Minister for Communications, Information Technology and the Arts, Senator Richard Alston, through the National Office for the Information Economy (NOIE) has not played any significant role in cryptographic policy formation. The Minister has recently (December 1998) issued a document, "A Strategic Framework for the Information Economy", which makes only minor reference to encryption issues. Australia was represented at the recent Wassenaar meetings by the Defense Department and the Department of Foreign Affairs and Trade, the latter being yet another player in policy formation.

In December 1996, Australia amended its export control laws to allow a personal-use exemption for encryption software that remains in the control of Australian users.

The Walsh Report recommends that Australia not establish a key escrow or recovery scheme as advocated by the United States. Its finding on this subject is as follows:

> 1.2.5 The Review does not support legislative action at this stage to prescribe a form of key management infrastructure accessible by government for purposes of national safety.
>
> 1.2.8 The Review does not recommend specific options for encryption legislation at this time.

1.2.11 There seems no compelling reason or virtue to move early on regulation or legislation concerning cryptography. Law enforcement and national security agencies have certainly experienced difficulty where subjects of investigation have refused access to encrypted stored data and it has not been possible for them or other agencies to decrypt this material. It is questionable, though, whether any range of policy decisions concerning key management would have altered this situation materially. For the present, the investigative capability of the agencies is not significantly affected.

1.2.27 Invocation of the principle of non self-incrimination is likely to prove an obstacle to efforts by law enforcement agencies to obtain encryption keys by search warrants or orders made by courts and tribunals.

1.2.39 The ready availability of strong encryption, with no requirement to escrow or register keys, nor to entrust them to any independent entity, is the most effective safeguard of individual privacy.

1.2.50 It would be premature to enter formal negotiations with other countries on access to encrypted data, where public keys are held in those countries, until there is some certainty as to likely key management infrastructures.

1.2.53 There is a high risk of corruption in the third party service provider sector and the Government would be prudent to require integrity screening and registration of those who seek to offer such services to the public.

1.2.56 There seems to be little popular support in or outside the United States for a 'Commercial Key Escrow' system involving government agencies creating as it would significant vulnerability outside of the control of the person or corporation.

In January 1999, an unredacted version of the Walsh Report was discovered by EFA and published on the Internet. Although Australia reported to the OECD that it imposes no import controls or domestic use controls on the use of cryptography, the redacted Walsh Report indicates changes have been recommended to these policies. These recommendations indicate that certain

Australian government agencies were entertaining methods for accessing plain text data that went beyond key escrow or recovery solutions:

> 1.2.28 The Crimes Act 1914 should be amended to permit the AFP, NCA and ASIO to 'hack' into a nominated computer system to secure access to that system or evidence of an electronic attack on a computer system.
>
> 6.2.3. The capacity to 'hack,' under a Justice of the Peace or Magistrate's warrant, would harmonize the search provision of the Crimes Act 1914 to today's standard form of storage.
>
> 6.3.3 It would seem sensible to coordinate work on profitable areas of technical attack among and between the investigative agencies, DSD and the Defense Science and Technology Organization (DSTO). Again the forum would be able to provide the requisite level of coordination.
>
> 1.2.33 Authority should be created for the AFP, the NCA and ASIO to alter proprietary software so that it performs additional functions to those specified by the manufacturer. Such an authority, which clearly should be subject to warranting provisions, would, for example, enable passive access to a computer work station of a LAN and link investigative capability more effectively to current technology. While there are issues of liability, the Review is convinced the effort should be made to accommodate these so that a target computer may be converted to a listening device. This capacity may represent one of the important avenues of accessing plain text.
>
> 6.2.10. The opportunity may present itself to the AFP, NCA or ASIO to alter software located in premises used by subjects of intensive investigation or destined to be located in those premises. The software (or more rarely the hardware) may relate to communication, data storage, encoding, encryption or publishing devices. While some modifications may have the effect of creating a listening device which may be remotely monitored by means of the telecommunications service, for which purposes extant warranting provisions would provide, others may create an intelligent memory, a permanent set of commands not specified in the program written by

> the manufacturer or a remote switching device with a capacity to issue commands at request. The cooperation of manufacturers or suppliers may sometimes be obtained by agencies. When manufacturers or suppliers are satisfied the modification has no discernible effect on function, they may consent to assist or acquiesce in its installation. It will not always be possible, however, to approach manufacturers or suppliers or the latter may be in no position to consent to modification of proprietary software. When agencies are investigating a high priority target, practicing effective personal and physical security, moving premises and changing telephone/fax regularly, an opportunity to access the target's computer equipment may represent not only the sole avenue but potentially the most productive.

There is also a candid admission that access to encrypted voice communications is desired more for intelligence-gathering purposes than for criminal investigations:

> 3.6.1 Little evidence emerges of encrypted voice communications being employed by criminal elements, although ASIO noted foreign intelligence services had long adopted the practice. Great weight was placed by those law enforcement agencies consulted and ASIO on the tactical importance of real-time access to voice and data communications for the conduct of investigations and the collection of evidence. It was said, and examples were advanced to support the contention, that loss of this access would seriously impact on their investigative capability. The unique advantages of interception of communications are passivity, flexibility and the low risk of the endeavor, combined with immediacy of intelligence flow. Denied this tool, agencies would be forced to engage in a wider range of human source activities, for which the preparatory planning stage is quite long, which may entail considerable financial outlays and about which there would be a high degree of operational, bureaucratic and political risk.

Australian legislation controlling the export of cryptography products has existed since at least 1987 when Australia became a member of COCOM. Cryptographic products require Ministry of Defense approval under Regulation 13B and the associated Schedule 13 of the Customs (Prohibited Exports) Regulations. As such, Australian export control regulations exceed the former Wassenaar guidelines in some areas, most notably in requiring individual export licensing for mass-market applications software and other mass-market software performing cryptographic functions. The new Wassenaar controls announced in December 1998 align Wassenaar more closely with Australia's long standing policy. A new Defense Strategic Goods List (DSGL) should be published in early 1999, following the December 1998 Wassenaar changes. The changes are expected to simplify applications for export of weak encryption products.

Approval or denial of export applications is based on economic factors, the impact on Australian national security, the identification of end users, and international obligations. Australia's guidelines for export licenses are not publicly available. Applications for export of cryptographic equipment are referred to the DSD for technical advice on the impact of exports on national security. DSD is the agency responsible for collecting foreign signals intelligence (SIGINT), much of which is shared with the U.S. National Security Agency under the terms of the UK-USA Security Agreement of 1948. DSD is also the agency responsible for the security of all Australian government communications.

As of January 1999, DSD remains responsible for evaluating license applications, but export policy is largely determined by the Defense Acquisition Organization, specifically the Director General for Exports and International Programs, a branch of the Defense Department. The Attorney General's department is responsible for legal aspects of security and encryption policy.

There are also redacted passages in the Walsh Report that emphasize the weaknesses inherent in export controls:

> 1.2.60 The continuing efficacy of export controls as a defensive strategy is dubious when no import controls exist and firms are able to evade the export controls of the United States, far and away the major software supplier, and purchase their requirements in Europe or Asia. As well, the Internet offers a marketplace without borders.
>
> 5.2.7 It has to be said the continuing validity of export controls as a defensive strategy is open to question when import controls do not exist in most countries, where firms in countries covered by multi-lateral agreements on the proliferation of cryptography are able to

circumvent United States' or Australia's export controls and buy the software of their choice in Asia or Europe and when easy access to the Internet is available to all.

Refs: Defense Signals Directorate letter dated January 14, 1999.
AG Letter Review of Policy relating to Encryption Technologies (Walsh Report), October 10, 1996.
http://www.efa.org.au/Issues/Crypto/Walsh/index.htm
http://zdnet.com.au /pcweek/content/1001/pcoz0004.html
E-mail dated January 21, 1999, Greg Taylor, Electronic Frontiers Australia.
OECD Group of Experts on Information Security and Privacy, Inventory of Controls on Cryptographic Technologies (DSTI/ICCP/REG(98)4/REV3), September 23, 1998.
http://www.dod.gov.au/dao/exportcontrols/greenbk/guidelin.htm
A Study of the International Market for Computer Software with Encryption , U.S. Department of Commerce and the National Security Agency, July 1995.

Austria

1999 GREEN/YELLOW
1998 YELLOW

Austria's report to the OECD indicates that in general there are no domestic controls on the use of cryptography (including transmissions over public telecommunications networks) or import restrictions.

On July 9, 1998, the Austrian Council of Ministers, the decision-making arm of the Federal government, accepted a revised draft report of the Federal Chancellery on encryption policy. The Council included a specific proviso that a draft statute must be tabled by the end of 1999, and this draft must comply in letter and spirit with six fundamental principles. These principles are taken directly from a Draft Digital Signatures and Cryptography Act that was tabled as a joint effort by a broad coalition of interests, including the Austrian Federation of Industrialists, the Austrian Chamber of Labour, various Federal Ministries and the two governing parties in parliament.

In paragraph 2 of the Draft Act, the government is explicitly enjoined from mandating a particular technology to end users. In addition, the use of key escrow is specifically prohibited. It also makes clear that all rules pertaining to setting up the infrastructure may not be used in any way to limit the use of technological means by everyone to achieve confidentiality and authenticity as she or he sees fit. The infrastructure envisioned may not be limited to authentication usage, but can also be applied for use in applications ensuring the confidentiality of communication.

The Federal Chancellery failed to submit the Draft Act to Parliament by the end of 1998 and drafting has now been delegated to the Ministry of Justice.

According to the Commerce/NSA report and the OECD Inventory of Controls on Cryptography Technologies, the Austrian government controls all encryption software as a dual-use item, and special licenses are required for its export, transit, or re-export. The legislation governing dual-use items is the Aussenhandelsgesetz 1995 BGBl 172/1995. The law implements the EU Dual Use Regulation 3381/94 and the Waasenaar Arrangement. Licenses are denied to destinations where an armed conflict is ongoing, to countries of concern, and to those against which there are international sanctions. Austria agreed to the enhanced Wassenaar controls announced in December 1998.

During our first survey, the Embassy of Austria in Washington, D.C. informed us that the Austrian organization responsible for cryptography usage and exports and imports was the Federal Ministry of Foreign Affairs, Section VI, in Vienna.

Ref: Embassy of Austria, Office of the Commercial Counselor fax dated June 24, 1997.
OECD Group of Experts on Information Security and Privacy, Inventory of Controls on Cryptographic Technologies (DSTI/ICCP/REG(98)4/REV3), September 23, 1998.
A Study of the International Market for Computer Software with Encryption , U.S. Department of Commerce and the National Security Agency, July 1995.
http://www.iaik.tu-graz.ac.at/LEHRE/StudProj/HAINZSILLI/crypto.ak.home.html/
Viktor Mayer-Schönberger / Michael Pilz / Christian Reiser / Gabriele Schmölzer, The Austrian Draft Digital Signatures Act, The Computer Law & Security Report Vol. 14 no. 5 (1998), 317.

Bahrain

1999 UNKNOWN
1998 UNKNOWN

During our first survey, we were contacted by telephone by the Embassy of Bahrain in Washington, D.C. and informed that the agency in Manama, Bahrain that was responsible for regulating the use of cryptography was the Directorate of Islamic Affairs, a component of the Ministry of Justice and Islamic Affairs. A direct query to that agency went unanswered.

Belarus

1999 RED
1998 RED

Belarus restricts the manufacture, maintenance, and use of cryptographic products. Licenses are required by the State Security Committee (the Belarussian KGB).

Ref: http://www.iaik.tu-graz.ac.at/LEHRE/StudProj/HAINZSILLI/crypto.ak.home.html

Belgium

1999 GREEN/YELLOW
1998 GREEN

There are no domestic controls on cryptography. In December 1994, the Belgian parliament enacted a law that would have required escrowed encryption. The law authorized the Belgian Institute for Posts and Telecommunications to establish a mandatory key escrow deposit system. The law contained homologation provisions that permitted the Belgacom to disconnect a phone that used unescrowed encryption. The law was rescinded by the Law of December 19, 1997 that created a new Article on the Law of March 21, 1991. The article provides that "the use of cryptography shall remain free from restrictions." The law permits cryptographic techniques to be used within the private domain, private enterprises, and private networks.

A draft law on computer crime would authorize the Public Prosecutor to require a criminal suspect to decrypt a message for the prosecutor to read when so ordered.

Belgium requires those wishing to export cryptography to countries other than the Netherlands and Luxembourg to first obtain an export license. This is contained in the Law of August 5, 1991 and the Royal Decree of March 8, 1993 regarding the import, export, and transmission of arms, munitions, and materials for military use and related technology. The European Union EU Dual Use Regulation 3381/94 has liberalized these requirements to cover additional EU members and certain non-EU countries. However an export license for exporting cryptographic hardware or software outside the BENELUX countries is still required. These liberalized EU provisions are contained in the ministerial decree of May 19, 1995. Belgium agreed to the enhanced Wassenaar controls announced in December 1998.

The agency in charge of approving export licenses is the A.R.E., 4th Division.

Ref: http://www.iaik.tu-graz.ac.at/LEHRE/StudProj/HAINZSILLI/crypto.ak.home.html
http://www.freenix.fr/netizen/20 5-e.html
OECD Group of Experts on Information Security and Privacy, Inventory of Controls on Cryptographic Technologies (DSTI/ICCP/REG(98)4/REV3), September 23, 1998.

Belize

1999 GREEN
1998 GREEN

The Embassy of Belize in Washington, D.C. informed us that they were not aware of any laws in Belize concerning the use of cryptography. They did inform us that cryptography was under the jurisdiction of the Attorney General's Ministry in Belmopan.

Ref: Embassy of Belize fax dated June 20, 1997.

Brazil

1999 GREEN/YELLOW
1998 GREEN

Brazil does not regulate the export, import or domestic use of encryption. However, there are indications that this situation may be changing. The Brazilian government is considering a law that would require importers and domestic users of encryption to register their products and systems with the government.

The PGP encryption program in Portuguese is available from Brazil via the Internet. The web site is http://www.dca.fee.unicamp.br/pgp.

Ref: NIST Preliminary Results of Study of Non - U.S. Cryptography Laws/Regulations, September 27, 1993.
White House Press Release, September 16, 1998.

Bulgaria

1999 GREEN/YELLOW
1998 GREEN/YELLOW

There are no domestic or import controls on the use of cryptography.

Bulgaria has acceded to the Wassenaar Arrangement and is presumably committed to restricting the export of cryptographic-enabled software as a dual-use good. Bulgaria agreed to the enhanced Wassenaar controls announced in December 1998.

Cambodia

1999 UNKNOWN

1998 UNKNOWN

During our first survey, the Embassy of Cambodia in Washington, D.C. informed us that although they were not aware of any laws concerning the use of cryptography in Cambodia, the Ministry with responsibility was the Ministry of Posts and Telecommunications in Phnom Penh. There was no response to our fax to the agency.

Ref: Royal Embassy of Cambodia fax dated June 19, 1997.

Campione d'Italia

1999 GREEN
1998 GREEN

Campione d'Italia is a small Italian enclave on the shores of Lake Lugano. It is totally surrounded by Switzerland. Although technically part of Italy's province of Como, its close affiliation with Switzerland, a non-member of the European Union, has made it a virtual "neutral zone" from European laws, including those dealing with taxation. A company developing encryption in this feudal anomaly would face little or no export restrictions because Campione's border with Switzerland is open (there is also unrestricted access to Liechtenstein) and Swiss laws do not apply in the enclave. Italy chooses not to apply most Italian laws dealing with financial regulations to the enclave. There is full Internet access via the modern Swiss PTT network. Because Campione has attracted numerous companies and banks, Italy prefers not to apply its laws to the territory.

Ref: www.henley-partner.com/campione.htm

Canada

1999 GREEN
1998 GREEN/YELLOW

There are no laws restricting the private use of cryptography. Canada's homologation regulations require that cryptographic equipment conform to public network technical requirements.

In October 1998, Minister of Industry John Manley announced the elements of Canada's Cryptography Policy. The policy is a component of the Canadian Electronic Commerce Strategy. The policy permits Canadians to develop, import and use whatever cryptography products they wish and does not impose mandatory key recovery requirements or a licensing regime. Manley stated that "This policy is good for the Canadian economy . . . It supports the increased use of electronic commerce products and services in Canada, as well as the export of Canadian information technologies to other countries."

The government said it believed it had achieved a balanced approach that encourages the growth of electronic commerce while maintaining the capability of law enforcement and national security agencies to ensure public safety.

Somewhat echoing his colleagues south of the border, Solicitor General Andy Scott said "Law enforcement agencies recognize the benefits of cryptography in protecting sensitive information . . . However, cryptography can also be used to shield criminal activities. This policy highlights the development of a framework to help law enforcement agencies deal with the challenges posed by advanced communications and information technologies, including cryptography."

Specifically, the Canadian government implemented a cryptography policy that:

- encourages the growth of electronic commerce;
- allows Canadian producers to export their products globally within the framework of international arrangements; and
- contains measures to maintain the capability of law enforcement agencies to ensure public safety.

The policy stipulates that:

- Canadians are free to develop, import and use whatever cryptography products they wish.

- The Government will not implement mandatory key recovery requirements or licensing regimes.

- The Government encourages industry to establish responsible practices, such as key recovery techniques for stored data.

- The Government will act as a model user of cryptography through the practices of the Government of Canada Public Key Infrastructure (GOC PKI).

- The Government encourages and supports industry-led accreditation of private sector certification authorities.

- Canada will continue to implement cryptography export controls in keeping with the framework of the international Wassenaar Arrangement. Canada will take into consideration the export practices of other countries and the availability of comparable products when rendering export permit decisions.

- The export permit application process will be made more transparent and procedures will be streamlined to ensure the least regulatory intervention necessary.

- The Government proposes amendments to the Criminal Code and other statutes as necessary to:

    - criminalize the wrongful disclosure of keys;
    - deter the use of encryption in the commission of a crime;
    - deter the use of cryptography to conceal evidence;
    - apply existing interception, search and seizure and assistance procedures
    - to cryptographic situations and circumstances.

Furthermore, the Government of Canada proposes to make it an offense to wrongfully disclose private encryption key information and to use cryptography to commit or hide evidence of a crime.

Canada was a member of COCOM and continues to adhere to the Wassenaar Arrangement, including the December 1998 changes to the export control lists. Consequently, Canada has issued guidelines for the export of information security related equipment and technologies that are reflected in hardware and software dual-use list found in the Export Control List. These export controls are authorized by the Export and Import Permits Act. Accordingly, export licenses are required for export to all destinations except the United States. One exception is for Canadian residents who are traveling temporarily away from Canada and may wish to take a portable personal computer containing encryption software. All U.S.-origin encryption products are also controlled under Canadian regulations and they also require an individual or general export permit. All types of Canadian-manufactured cryptography can be exported freely from Canada to the United States. Canada regulates all types of exports of cryptography, including tangible (physical diskette) and intangible form (products downloaded from the Internet). When specific requests for export of intangibles are received, they are assessed on an individual basis.

There have been statements that the Canadian government will not impose strict new rules for export controls following the December Wassenaar changes. According to Canadian officials, mass-market software with encryption with a bit length of 128 bits will only require a one-time general license. Public domain software will not require any license.

The Foreign Affairs Export Controls Division of the Department of Foreign Affairs and International Trade works closely with Canada's Communications Security Establishment (CSE), the NSA's Canadian SIGINT partner, regarding export decisions on cryptographic products. The Division stated that the CSE works closely with the NSA, the UK's Government Communications Headquarters (GCHQ), and Australia's DSD on cryptographic export policies. Canada reported to the OECD that export permits are assessed on a routine basis for multiple destination countries or end-users for encryption products with key lengths of 56-bit DES equivalent or less. These are subject to a one-time review. Permits are also eased for trusted end-users, particularly Canadian corporations or bona fide financial institutions.

Ref: OECD Group of Experts on Information Security and Privacy, Inventory of Controls on Cryptographic Technologies (DSTI/ICCP/REG(98)4/REV3), September 23, 1998.

Press Release 8099-e, Office of the Minister of Industry, October 1, 1998, <http://info.ic.gc.ca/cmb/welcomeic.nsf/261ce500dfcd7259852564820068dc 6d/85256613004a2e1785256690004c70fb?OpenDocument>
A Study of the International Market for Computer Software with Encryption , U.S. Department of Commerce and the National Security Agency, July 1995.
E-Mail, Industry Canada, February 1, 1999.

Chile

1999 GREEN
1998 Not reported

There are reportedly no prohibitions on the export, import, or domestic use of cryptographic products in Chile.

Ref: http://cwis.kub.nl/~frw/people/koops/cls2.htm#bi

China

1999 RED
1998 RED

According to the NIST survey, China practices a licensing system for the use, importing and exporting of various commodities, including encryption hardware and software. An application must be filed and a license obtained in advance by corporations approved by the State to engage in the business of importing and exporting encryption products. The licenses are valid for one year and extensions may be applied for.

The Notice of the General Administration of Customs of the People's Republic of China, Sec. 50-305, of November 1, 1987 (List of Prohibited and Restricted Imports and Exports), restricts the import and export of voice-encoding devices.

Corporations engaging in the export business must file an approval application with the Ministry of Foreign Trade and Economic Cooperation or the foreign trade bureau of the particular province. The Ministry establishes an export control list of prohibited and restricted goods. These regulations are contained in Interim Procedures of the State Import-Export Commission and Ministry of Foreign Trade of the People's Republic of China Concerning the System of Export Licensing of June 3, 1980.

Ref: NIST Preliminary Results of Study of Non - U.S. Cryptography Laws/Regulations, September 27, 1993.

Croatia

1999 GREEN
1998 GREEN

According to the Ministry of Science and Technology, there are no domestic use, import or export controls for encryption in Croatia. There is also no agency in charge of setting policy.

On September 16, 1998, the United States authorized the export of unlimited strength encryption products (with or without key recovery) to the banking and financial, insurance, health and medical, and on-line electronic commercial sectors in Croatia. This is an indication that the U.S. has leveraged its authority to gain access to plain text information in those sectors within the country under Mutual Legal Assistance Treaty (MLAT)/Financial Action Task Force (FATF) provisions. Interestingly, Croatia is not eligible for a U.S. Encryption Licensing Agreement for the export of recoverable products, an indication that the U.S. does not entirely trust the Croatian intelligence service and law enforcement agencies from abusing third party access to keys.

Ref: Email communication from Ministry of Science and Technology, Feb. 9, 1999.
White House Press Announcement, September 16, 1998.

Cyprus

1999 GREEN
1998 GREEN/YELLOW

According to the Cyprus Telecommunications Authority, there are no domestic use controls, export controls or import controls on cryptographic products in Cyprus. In addition, no government agency has established authority over cryptographic policy.

Ref: E-Mail, Cyprus Telecommunications Authority, Lefkosia, Cyprus, January 12, 1999.

Czech Republic

1999 GREEN/YELLOW
1998 GREEN/YELLOW

There are no domestic prohibitions on the use of cryptography in the Czech Republic.

The Czech Republic enacted a decree known as the "Control of Exports and Imports of Goods Subject to International Control Regimes". The decree incorporates both the EU and Wassenaar lists of controlled dual-use lists into Czech export law. The Czech Republic is a Participating State in Wassenaar and a candidate for EU membership.

The Ministry of Industry and Trade reviews the exports of cryptographic product. The Ministry will issue either an individual license or an individual open license for exports. An individual license is for a one-time export of a cryptographic product while an individual open license covers recurring exports of cryptographic products for a particular destination and for a finite period of time. The export law of the Czech Republic covers only tangible cryptographic products.

The Czech Republic also extends its export law to the import of cryptographic products. Although the Ministry of Industry and Trade retains authority to control imports, it has issued a general import license for cryptographic products and users do not require any special authorization to bring such products into the Czech Republic.

On December 31, 1998, the United States authorized the export of unlimited strength encryption products (with or without key recovery) to the banking and financial sectors in the Czech Republic. This is an indication that the U.S. has leveraged its authority to gain access to plain text information in those sectors within the country under Mutual Legal Assistance Treaty (MLAT)/Financial Action Task Force (FATF) provisions.

Ref: A Study of the International Market for Computer Software with Encryption , U.S. Department of Commerce and the National Security Agency, July 1995.
OECD Group of Experts on Information Security and Privacy, Inventory of Controls on Cryptographic Technologies (DSTI/ICCP/REG(98)4/REV3), September 23, 1998.

Denmark

1999 GREEN/YELLOW
1998 GREEN

Denmark reported to the OECD that there are no domestic use prohibitions on the use of cryptography in Denmark.

In April 1997, an Export Committee on Cryptography, meeting under the auspices of the Ministry of Research and Technology and including representatives of other ministries, issued a report on the use and sale of cryptographic products. The Committee recommended that Denmark not impose new regulations on cryptography. However, it did state that Danish cryptography policy should take into consideration international developments (an obvious reference to Wassenaar and other regimes). The Committee particularly recommended against the establishment in Denmark of a key recovery scheme. In June 1998, the Committee issued its final recommendation. Although the Committee recommended that key recovery regulations and incentive schemes should not be implemented, international developments might necessitate a reconsideration of such controls in the future.

Denmark has implemented Wassenaar export controls in its Executive Order on Exports of Dual-Use Goods Technologies and Know-how. Denmark adheres to the amended Wassenaar Dual-Use Control list agreed to in Vienna in December 1998. This has caused some political controversy in Denmark and hearings may be held in the Parliament this year.

The Danish Agency for Trade and Industry licenses exports of cryptographic products. Danish export controls cover both tangible and intangible software transfers. Criminal sanctions can be levied against those who illegally transfer unlicensed cryptographic products subject to export controls. The Danish Defense Intelligence Service (*Forsvarets Efterretningstjeneste*) determines what and to whom cryptographic products may be exported.

Denmark originally regulated the export of strategic goods under a Ministry of Industry executive order dated November 12, 1993. The executive order has been subsumed by the EU dual-use regulation.

Ref: OECD Group of Experts on Information Security and Privacy, Inventory of Controls on Cryptographic Technologies (DSTI/ICCP/REG(98)4/REV3), September 23, 1998.
No Regulation of Cryptography Now, Press release 27.05.97 <http://www.fsk.dk/fsk/presse/97/970527.html>
A Study of the International Market for Computer Software with Encryption , U.S. Department of Commerce and the National Security Agency, July 1995.

Dominica

1999 GREEN
1998 Not reported

According to Delphis Ltd., a major Internet Service Provider in Dominica, there are no domestic use prohibitions, export or import controls on cryptography in Dominica. In addition, no government agency has been charged with regulating cryptographic technology.

On September 16, 1998, the United States authorized the export of unlimited strength encryption products (with or without key recovery) to the banking and financial, insurance, health and medical, and on-line electronic commercial sectors in Dominica. This is an indication that the U.S. has leveraged its authority to gain access to plain text information in those sectors within the country under Mutual Legal Assistance Treaty (MLAT)/Financial Action Task Force (FATF) provisions.

Ref: E-Mail, Delphis Ltd., Roseau, Commonwealth of Dominica, January 11, 1999.
White House Press Release, September 16, 1998.

Estonia

1999 GREEN
1998 GREEN

The Estonian government, in formulating its cryptographic policy, has recommended that the main principles approved by the OECD, EU, and other organizations will be accepted. Therefore, the use of cryptographic algorithms and methods will be free and no key escrow systems or other limitations for cryptographic systems will be introduced in Estonia. The ministry responsible for regulating cryptography use is the Estonian State Secretary. Estonians therefore have the right to import and use encryption products in the country.

NATO representatives have reportedly pressured Estonia to adopt key recovery schemes as a pre-condition for joining the Western alliance. However, the EU has rejected the key recovery approach and Germany, in particular, is said to have warned Estonia that it would have to adopt the EU policy on cryptography before joining the Union.

As Estonia is a candidate for full membership in the EU, it has adopted the EU's dual-use control list for cryptographic exports. Accordingly, exports require a license from the Ministry of Foreign Affairs.

Ref: Dr. Monika Oit and Valdo Praust, "The Estonian view on National Information Security Policy," Baltic IT&T '98, Riga, Latvia, April 15-18, 1998.
"U.S. Assault on Northern Europe," *Intelligence Newsletter*, No. 342, September 17, 1998.

Falkland Islands

1999 GREEN
1998 GREEN

According to Mr. D. G. Lang, the Attorney General of the Falkland Islands, there are no laws in the sparsely populated British territory that specifically deal with the use of cryptography. Mr. Lang informed us that, as Attorney General, he does have legitimate concerns about the possible use of cryptography by criminal organizations in furtherance of international crime or terrorism. However, he said that there is no organized crime on the islands. He did offer his belief that the Falklands government is committed to joining the international effort to combat organized crime and, if the international community were to launch an effort against the use of "uncrackable" cryptography, the Falklands would join in such an effort.

According to the Attorney General, although the Falklands has a Constitutional guarantee respecting the privacy of the individual, this guarantee falls short of an absolute guarantee of privacy. An individual, in the Attorney General's opinion, would probably be unsuccessful in challenging on Constitutional grounds a possible future provision prohibiting or restricting his or her use of cryptographic techniques.

The Attorney General stated that cryptography is used in the Falklands for both business and government operations. He is not opposed to usage by such organizations, but merely the use of cryptography by criminals for criminal purposes.

Since United Kingdom laws do not automatically apply to the territories, the response of the Falkland Islands Attorney General is significant.

Ref: Attorney General of the Falkland Islands letter dated July 3, 1997.

Finland

1999 GREEN/YELLOW
1998 GREEN

A new Finnish Cryptographic Policy was announced on January 5, 1999:

The Government of Finland adheres to the following guidelines concerning the national cryptography policy and statements on the use of cryptographic products:

- At the national level, Finland supports free trade and use of cryptographic products. In Finland, the use of strong encryption should not be restricted by legislation or international agreements.

- With regard to exports and export restrictions, Finland observes those arrangements to which it is internationally committed. However, with regard to reform of control lists and procedures Finland's aims are to examine the restrictions on cryptographic products so that control lists correspond to technical development, and to ensure that the necessary restrictions will not unreasonably impede normal foreign trade of industry and businesses. The administration of foreign affairs takes the view that it is important that Government cryptography policy or public discussion of it does not impair the international credibility of the export controls maintained by Finland.

- The license and other authorization systems applicable to the provision of cryptography services and safe certification services needed for user identification are created by legislation. The systems have to be simple and based on voluntary action. Users are informed about the dangers related to the disappearance of the secret keys used in the encryption of data, and they are encouraged to use safe key management systems and other certification services. Saving the secret keys used in encryption for use by the authorities will not be made mandatory by law. No copies of the secret keys needed to produce electronic signatures will be kept.

- For the purposes of crime investigation, the authorities have the power, under the Pre-Trial Investigation Act and Coercive Criminal

Investigation Means Act, to obtain a telecommunications message from the sender or the receiver. However, a crime suspect has no obligation to assist in the decryption of an encrypted telecommunications message or data saved in encrypted form. The authorities may demand the provider of certification services or the maintainer of the encryption system to hand over a secret key in their possession or to otherwise contribute to the investigation of individual encrypted data according to the requirements of the Pre-Trial Investigation Act and Coercive Criminal Investigation Means Act. By December 31, 1998, the Ministry of Justice of Finland, together with the Ministry of the Interior of Finland, will clarify the need to reform the Coercive Criminal Investigation Means Act from the criminal investigation viewpoint of cryptographic products.

- The Council of State will promote the development of electronic signature, electronic services and safe cryptographic products and cryptography services by a positive and open attitude towards the use of these services and products and by defining and creating the user identification solutions and certification services needed by the administration.

According to the Ministry of Trade and Industry of Finland:

- Finland has implemented no specific legislation on the domestic use of cryptographic software and hardware. There are no special permit requirements in this respect.
- Finland has implemented no specific legislation on the import of cryptographic software and hardware. There are no import license requirements.

Finland's national legislation relevant to export controls are:

- Act on the Control of Exports of Dual-Use Goods (562/96).
- Decree on Export Control of Certain Goods (645/96).
- Decision of the Ministry of Trade and Industry on the Goods and Technologies Subject to Export Licensing (645/96).

The national legislation refers to the European export control systems which consists of two legal instruments:

- Council Regulation (EC) No. 3381/94 of 19 December 1994 setting up a Community regime for the control of exports of dual-use goods, with amendment (EC) No. 837/95.
- Council Decision 94/942/CFSP of 19 December 1994 on the joint action adopted by the council on the basis of Article J.3 of the Treaty on European Union concerning the control of exports of dual-use goods (with several amendments - the latest relevant amendment concerning the controls on intra-Community trade of cryptography is 97/419/CFSP of 26 June 1997).

The EU Regulation is directly applicable to all the Member States of the European Union. Finland's control lists (including definitions, general notes, etc.) concerning the export control of cryptographic software and hardware are identical to those agreed to in the Wassenaar Arrangement and the European Union Treaty. The only relevant difference to the controls maintained by the EU is that Finland's national legislation also covers the export of services, including the transfer of intangible technology, e.g., via electronic mail. Finland adheres to the revised Wassenaar Dual-Use Control List agreed to in Vienna in December 1998.

In an interview with the Finnish national newspaper *Helsingin Sanomat* (December 15, 1998), Finnish Prime Minister Paavo Lipponen claimed it was the "very powerful position of the United States" that forced through the changes to Wassenaar. He added, "the Wassenaar negotiations are highly secret." The Prime Minister, noting that the controls could hurt Finnish industry, stated, "Finland still aims for openness and free markets also in this area." Lipponen had to consider the position of Nokia, a Finnish firm with a large market share of the international cellular telephone market and Data Fellows, a cryptographic firm that has enjoyed 90-120 per cent annual growth including a significant international market share. Nokia's trade policy director, told *Helsingin Sanomat* that along with other industry sectors, his firms believes that strong encryption should be permitted and its export should not be restricted. He said applying for export restrictions creates additional work and costs and the process is a "difficult thing."

The government agencies responsible for setting policies on the use, importation, and exportation of cryptographic products include the Ministry of Trade and Industry and the Ministry for Foreign Affairs for export controls and electronic commerce, and the Ministry of Communications, and the Security Police (SUPO) (a component of the Interior Ministry). The

Ministry of Finance has started a survey on the need for national information security legislation, including a law on digital signatures. Their work is ongoing.

Ref: Ministry of Trade and Industry, Helsinki, fax dated July 28, 1997.
National cryptography policy, October 1998
<http://www.vn.fi/lm/telecom/cryptography/guidelines.htm>
OECD Group of Experts on Information Security and Privacy, Inventory of Controls on Cryptographic Technologies (DSTI/ICCP/REG(98)4/REV3), September 23, 1998.

France

1999 YELLOW/GREEN
1998 RED/YELLOW

France made a significant change in policy since our first survey in 1998. On January 19, 1999, Prime Minister Lionel Jospin announced a dramatic cryptography policy change. The new policy abolishes France's complex licensing scheme for cryptographic imports and domestic use, mandatory key registration requirements for the domestic use of encryption, and a system of government-approved trusted third parties.

On January 19, Jospin stated:

> The Government allowed itself time to reflect. After consulting those involved, experts and international partners, it became convinced that the dispositions which result from the law of 1996 are no longer appropriate. They strictly restrain the use of encryption in France, without allowing the authorities to efficiently combat criminal acts where encoding could facilitate dissimulation. They also make apparent a risk of isolation for France with regard to her main partners.
>
> The Government has therefore decided to opt for a fundamental change of direction, which aims to make the use of encryption totally permitted in France, while adapting the means at the disposal of the

authorities to guarantee public liberty in this new environment and to combat the use of encoding methods for illicit ends.

The draft bill that will be presented to Parliament will be based on the following orientations:

- provide total freedom of use of encryption products, with one restraint to maintain control over exports which result from France's international engagements (encoding methods that do not use keys that are longer than 56 bits);

- suppress the mandatory nature of having recourse to a third party of confidence for depositing encoding keys. The role of the third party will not be limited to managing keys but can extend to other tasks, such as certifying electronic signatures. Recourse to such instruments and to auto-depository mechanisms will be encouraged. The third parties of confidence can notably apply for certification from the authorities.

- allow the authorities to efficiently combat the use of encoding procedures for illicit ends. To this end, the current legal mechanism will be supplemented by setting up obligations, as well as penal sanctions, with regard to presenting the uncoded transcription of encoded documents to the legal authorities when they so request. Moreover, the technical capacities of the authorities will be significantly reinforced.

The law, therefore, must be changed, which will take several months. But the Government wished that the hindrances which handicap citizens who are anxious to protect the confidentiality of their exchanges, and the development of electronic commerce, be lifted without delay. Thus, while waiting for the legislative modifications announced, the Government decided to raise the threshold for permitted encryption methods from 40 bits to 128 bits, a level which is considered by experts to resolutely ensure high security.

As far as the supply of encryption products is concerned, the declaration procedure will be simplified, notably through the suppression of the simple stop test. Finally, the constraints on the third parties of confidence that can be modified through regulatory means will be considerably relaxed, in particular by the suppression of the requirement for defense clearance for personnel and 24 hour per day availability.

In March 1999 the French government announced three decrees that are intended to relax controls on encryption. The *Service Central de la Sécurité des Systèmes d'Information* (SCSSI) is the regulatory body in France as far as cryptography is concerned. SCSSI comes under the authority of the Secretary General for National Defense (SGDN) and has a direct reporting line to the office of the Prime Minister of France. French cryptography controls are much more stringent than those recommended by the Wassenaar Arrangement, of which France is a party. In December 1998, France subscribed to the more restrictive Wassenaar Dual-Use Control List. French export control laws do not distinguish between tangible and intangible cryptographic products. The Commerce/NSA report states that "France has the most comprehensive cryptologic control and use regime in Europe, and possibly worldwide."

France's report to the OECD states that export, import, and domestic use controls on the use of encryption in France prior to Prime Minister Jospin's announcement were governed by:

- Law 90-1170 of December 29, 1990, Article 28, modified by law 91-648 of July 11, 1991; and further modified by law 96-659 of July 26, 1996, particularly article 17 on criminal penalties. The July 26, 1996 law, Article 17, stipulates that the sale, import from non-EU nations, and export of cryptographic devices or services are subject to government authorization if its performs confidentiality functions. The authorization, if provided, will either be a general authorization (i.e., an authorization to supply or export devices to any user), or a private use authorization which restricts supply, export, or use to specifically named individuals or communities. Data that is submitted by the supplier, user, or exporter in order to obtain such authorization is extensive. In general, the information submitted must "describe not only the algorithm for generating a sequence or pseudo-random block, but all the hardware or software facilities, transforming an intelligible plain signal into an unintelligible cryptogram, including generating keys, storing them, managing them, etc." This created a Trusted Third Party System that was never implemented.
- Decree 95-613 of May 5, 1995 on exports of dual-use goods.

- Order of May 5, 1995 on exports of dual-use goods to third party countries and European Union Member States.
- Order of May 5, 1995 defining the general G.502 license for exporting encryption products, including the granting and use of the license.
- Decree 96-67 of January 29, 1996 on the responsibilities of the SGDN on information technology security.
- Decree 98-101 of February 24, 1998 defining the conditions under which declarations are submitted and licenses granted for the import, export, domestic use, and supply of encryption products. This decree restricted encryption imports into France, including those over the Internet.
- Decree 98-102 of February 1998 defining the conditions under which trusted third parties are licensed in accordance with Article 28 of Law 90-1170 of December 29, 1990 on telecommunications.

Ref: Interministerial Committee on the Information Society (CISI) - January 19th,1999. < http://www.premier-ministre.gouv.fr/GB/INFO/FICHE1GB.HTM>
http://www.iris.sgdg.org/axes/crypto
http://www.internet.gouv.fre
OECD Group of Experts on Information Security and Privacy, Inventory of Controls on Cryptographic Technologies (DSTI/ICCP/REG(98)4/REV3), September 23, 1998.
Embassy of France fax dated June 23, 1997.
A Study of the International Market for Computer Software with Encryption , U.S. Department of Commerce and the National Security Agency, July 1995.

Germany

1999 GREEN
1998 GREEN

Germany has been at the forefront of opposing restrictions on encryption. It has been a counter-balance to U.S. efforts to promote key escrow and international restrictions. It had a significant role in the EU's 1997 paper on Encryption and Digital Signatures. In 1999, German efforts prevented key escrow from becoming part of the Wassenaar Arrangement.

According to the Embassy of the Federal Republic of Germany in Washington and the Federal Ministry of Economics and Technology:

- There are no controls on the use of encryption software or hardware;
- There are no controls on the import of encryption;
- Export controls on encryption are comparable to those of the United States as they existed until early in 1997;
- Export controls are overseen by the Federal Exports Office of the Ministry of Economics (Bundesamt fuer Aussenwirtschaf- BMWi).

Germany enacted a Digital Signature Law (SigG) on June 11, 1997. The digital signature system mandated uses asymmetric encryption. This system requires a secret key to be held by the signer and a public key that is certified by a Certificate Authority. The encryption algorithm to be used is not defined in the law. The law does not specify Certificate Authorities, but it requires that such parties be licensed by the government communications authority. This authority will certify Certificate Authorities and create a digital chain of trust for purposes of public key verification.

According to Germany's report to the OECD, the "Electronic Commerce Initiative of the Federal Government" states that "the German government does not plan to regulate by statute the marketing and use of encryption products. In Germany, encryption systems may be freely chosen and used." In its progress report on the German action plan "Info 2000 – Germany's Way to an Information Society" (Autumn 1997), the government states its policy is to:

- Ensure availability of reliable and strong encryption in Germany on a sustainable basis;
- Guard the interests of German security and criminal prosecution authorities; and
- Promote the strength of the market position of German producers of encryption systems.

Cryptographic exports are regulated by the implementation of the EU Dual-Use Regulation. Encryption equipment is listed individually in the German export list (Appendix to the *Aussenwirtschaftsverordnung*) in Part 1 C, paragraph 5 part 2 "Information Security." In 1998, the German Green Party posed the following question to the Federal Government: "Is the Federal

Government aware of the view of cryptographic experts that certain encryption standards and systems have been watered down by the influence of agencies responsible for cryptography matters, in particular the NSA, and what is its response to this viewpoint?" The government's answer was surprisingly candid, "The restrictive export control policy of the USA with regard to encryption technology is generally known; in its advisory role the BSI (*Bündesamt fur Sicherheit der Informationstechnik* -- the German Federal Information Security Agency, a department of the Ministry of the Interior) is, therefore, cautious with regard to recommending U.S. products to the public administration and to private German companies."

In December 1998, Germany adhered to the revised Wassenaar Arrangement export controls, tightening up its own export criteria. However, the Ministry of Economics has indicated that they do not plan to impose new restrictions on the export of cryptographic products.

Ref: E-mail from the German Ministry of Economics and Technology, January 19, 1999.
Press Release of the German Federal Ministry of Economic Affairs, December 8, 1998 on Wassenaar Arrangement Export Control for Encryption Technology Relaxed: No Forthcoming "Key Recovery" for Crypto Products. <http://www.kuner.com/data/new/wassenaar.html>
OECD Group of Experts on Information Security and Privacy, Inventory of Controls on Cryptographic Technologies (DSTI/ICCP/REG(98)4/REV3), September 23, 1998.
Embassy of the Federal Republic of Germany fax dated June 19, 1997.
A Study of the International Market for Computer Software with Encryption, U.S. Department of Commerce and the National Security Agency, July 1995.

Gibraltar

1999 GREEN
1998 GREEN

The Gibraltar Government Mission in Washington did not respond to our survey. However, the government of this British self-governing territory on the southern tip of Spain hosts an Internet gaming site (called InterKeno). Registration is made via the Internet and credit card details submitted on heavily encrypted pages. The government of Gibraltar receives licensing fees from this operation and it is unlikely that they would support a form of key recovery or escrow which might result in disruption of the gaming operations.

Exports are regulated under the EU Dual Use restrictions.

Ref: http://www. bet4abetterworld.com/general/geninfo.html#Security Information

Greece

1999 GREEN/YELLOW
1998 GREEN/YELLOW

Greece reported to the OECD that there are no import or domestic controls on cryptography in Greece.

During our first survey, the Embassy of Greece in Washington informed us that Greece had no contemporary or projected legislation concerning the use, import, or export of cryptography.

In December 1998, Greece subscribed to the more restrictive Wassenaar Dual-Use Control List.

Also, see the entry for Mount Athos.

Ref: Embassy of Greece letter dated July 15, 1997.
OECD Group of Experts on Information Security and Privacy, Inventory of Controls on Cryptographic Technologies (DSTI/ICCP/REG(98)4/REV3), September 23, 1998.

Hong Kong

1999 YELLOW
1998 YELLOW

There are no domestic controls on encryption use in Hong Kong.

Import and export of cryptography is regulated by the Import and Export (Strategic Commodities) Regulations. Licenses are required for cryptography imports and exports. Authentication cryptography that is not used for confidentiality purposes is exempt from this requirement. Licenses for exports and imports are issued by the Department of Trade of the Special Administrative Region of Hong Kong. Import and export control lists mirror those of the Wassenaar Arrangement since Hong Kong is a cooperating party to the export control scheme.

On September 16, 1998, the United States authorized the export of unlimited strength encryption products (with or without key recovery) to the banking and financial, insurance, health and medical, and on-line electronic commercial sectors in Hong Kong. This is an indication that the U.S. has leveraged its authority to gain access to plain text information in those sectors within the country under Mutual Legal Assistance Treaty (MLAT)/Financial Action Task Force (FATF) provisions. Interestingly, Hong Kong is not eligible for a U.S. Encryption Licensing Agreement for the export of recoverable products, an indication that the U.S. does not entirely trust the Chinese intelligence services and both Hong Kong and Chinese law enforcement agencies from abusing third party access to keys.

Ref: http://cwis.kub.nl/~frw/people/koops/cls2.htm#bi
White House Press Announcement, September 16, 1998.

Hungary

1999 GREEN/YELLOW
1998 GREEN/YELLOW

There are no domestic controls on the use of cryptography in Hungary.

Hungary has implemented export controls on dual-use cryptography as required by the Wassenaar Arrangement, to which it is a party. In December 1998, Hungary subscribed to the more restrictive Wassenaar Dual-Use Control List. The Ministry of Economic Affairs licenses exports of encryption products. Import controls on cryptography also require a license in much the same manner as that applied to exports.

Ref: OECD Group of Experts on Information Security and Privacy, Inventory of Controls on Cryptographic Technologies (DSTI/ICCP/REG(98)4/REV3), September 23, 1998.

Iceland

1999 GREEN
1998 GREEN

Iceland's report to the OECD states that there are no restrictions on the import, export, or domestic use of cryptography in Iceland. The country is not a party to the Wassenaar Arrangement nor was it a member of its predecessor, COCOM.

Ref: OECD Group of Experts on Information Security and Privacy, Inventory of Controls on Cryptographic Technologies (DSTI/ICCP/REG(98)4/REV3), September 23, 1998.

India

1999 YELLOW/RED
1998 YELLOW/RED

According to a report written by the Information Technology Group, a component of the Department of Electronics of the Government of India, the cryptography situation in India largely remains in the development stage. Few organizations, including those in the defense sector, are engaged exclusively in the development of cryptography techniques, protocols and products. However, cryptographic products compatible with DOS and Windows environments have been developed and are being used commercially. Also, customized cryptographic products have been designed and produced for commercial use. The issue of public and private key usage is under the purview of the Joint Cipher Bureau, the agency responsible for handling all encryption-related technology in India.

Also according to the Department of Electronics report, the Department of Telecommunications does not permit encrypted signals to be transmitted over their network, but this does not appear to be enforced. Secondly, since cryptographic products world-wide are licensed items and licenses to India are not easily available for products of higher key lengths (greater than 56 bits), Indian industry largely produces PC software products containing cryptography at the 56-bit level. Stronger systems are not yet produced in India.

In 1998, the conservative Bharatiya Janata Party (BJP) government introduced the Indian Information Technology Act. The legislation would require all Internet Service Providers to monitor all traffic passing through their servers, making traffic, including the plain text of encrypted traffic, available to "properly constituted authorities" for "valid reasons of security." Properly constituted authorities include the Central Bureau of Investigation (CBI), the Intelligence Bureau (IB) and the Research and Analysis Wing (RAW).

India's concern about cryptography use stems in part from the fact that some insurgent groups have used the technology to protect their communications. In October 1998, the Governor of Maharashtra State displayed equipment captured from rebel groups in Kashmir. The equipment included "high-frequency radio transceivers" complete with "electronic ruggedized encryption keyboards that can cipher and decipher 45 characters at a time" and "modems to send and receive ciphered messages."

The Indian government requires cellular network operators to provide "monitoring facilities" to investigative agencies. The monitoring equipment, capable of providing "in clear" access to conversations, must be paid for by the cellphone companies.

According to the Commerce/NSA report, India has a formidable government structure that has exercised a great deal of control regulating foreign trade in items in short supply, rather than controlling defense-related exports for national security reasons. As of May 1994, India had no publicly available guidelines or formal licensing procedures governing exports of munitions or sensitive dual-use commodities. It was felt that all munitions and military items of concern were produced by defense factories that restricted their export. Therefore, India maintained no formal export licensing system for munitions items. In March 1995, India published a list of strategic raw materials and technologies that are subject to export licensing. The list controls equipment and software for encrypted telemetry systems only (missile technology controls form a major portion of the list). No encryption software is controlled by the list. This information was gleaned from State Department New Delhi Cables 8364, May 24, 1994 and 5852, May 3, 1995.

Under an Indo - U.S. memorandum of understanding on trade in sensitive technologies, the government of India has agreed to "facilitate" the import of items appearing on the U.S. Commodity Control List and the U.S. Munitions List. In January 1999, the Defense Research and Development Organization (DRDO) issued a 'red alert' against all network security software developed in the US. N. Vittal, the Commissioner of the Central Vigilance Center of the DRDO, said he was considering making it mandatory for all Indian banks and financial institutions to buy only security software developed in India.

Specifically, the DRDO is concerned about U.S. "encryption software products" that can be 'broken' by the NSA. The agency pointed out "no encryption software products can be exported from the U.S. if they are too strong to be broken by the U.S. National Security Agency." The quality of such software exported to India is therefore questionable from a security point of view. The DRDO claimed its own encryption has "no upper limit" and can be appended to software exported from the United States. The letter says: "To put it bluntly, only insecure software can be exported. When various multinational companies go around peddling 'secure communication software' products to gullible Indian customers, they conveniently neglect to mention this aspect of the U.S. export law."

Ref: Gulshan Rai, R.K.Dubash, and A.K.Chakravarti, "Cryptography Technology and Policy Directions in the Context of NII," Version 1, Cyberlaw Series 3, December 1997, Information Technology Group Dept. of Electronics Govt. of India <http://www.allindia.com/gov/doe/cryplaw.htm#index>.
"Arms from Kashmir draw crowds," *The Hindu*, October 23, 1998.
Ramesh Vinayak, "Punjab: Mobile Mischief," *India Today*, December 8, 1997, p. 49.
<http://www.arachnis.com/udhay/articles/art-activism2.html>
Mayur Shetty, "Red alert issued against U.S. network software," *Economic Times* (India) http://www.economictimes.com/120199/lead2.htm

A Study of the International Market for Computer Software with Encryption , U.S. Department of Commerce and the National Security Agency, July 1995.

Indonesia

1999 GREEN
1998 YELLOW

According to the Embassy of Indonesia in Washington, cryptography regulations for domestic use are an entirely new matter for that country. The Commercial Attaché in Washington has been keeping its parent organization in Jakarta informed of developments on the cryptographic front in the United States.

The embassy also informed us that the agency responsible for setting policy on cryptographic exports and imports is the Directorate General of International Trade, a component of the Ministry of Industry and Trade.

Ref: Embassy of the Republic of Indonesia, Office of the Commercial Attaché letter dated July 7, 1997.

Iran

1999 UNKNOWN
1998 UNKNOWN

The Interests Section of Iran at the Embassy of Pakistan in Washington, D.C. informed us that our request for information on encryption laws in Iran had been forwarded to "the appropriate organization in the Islamic republic of Iran to be reviewed." No further information was forthcoming.

Ref: Interests Section of the Islamic Republic of Iran, Embassy of Pakistan, Washington, D.C. letter dated July 7, 1997.

Ireland

1999 GREEN
1998 GREEN/YELLOW

There are neither domestic controls on cryptographic use nor any import restrictions of encryption technology in Ireland.

On June 24, 1998, the Irish government weighed in with a new cryptographic policy aimed at supporting companies like Baltimore Technologies and its competitors such as Systemics Ltd. of Dublin. The Irish government cryptography policy clearly rejects key escrow and recovery regimes in favor of court-ordered and warrant-based access to the plaintext of encrypted data. Ireland's policy is as follows:

> "Ireland's policy on the use of encryption technologies is based on the recognition that an effective policy should achieve a balance between the rights of the individual in regard to privacy, the need to provide for security and integrity of communications, the development of the cryptography industry in Ireland, and the requirements for lawful access to data for the purposes of law enforcement and national security. The policy comprises the following basic principles:
>
> - Users shall have the right to access strong and secure encryption to ensure the confidentiality, security and reliability of stored data and electronic communications.
>
> - Users shall have the right to choose any cryptographic method.
>
> - The production, import and use of encryption technologies in Ireland shall not be subject to any regulatory controls other than obligations relating to lawful access.
>
> - The export of cryptographic products is to continue to be regulated in accordance with the relevant EU Regulations and Decisions and Irish national legislation which reflect the Wassenaar Arrangement on Export Controls for Dual-Use Goods and Technologies and Conventional Arms.
>
> In order to enable lawful access to encrypted data, legislation will be enacted to oblige users of encryption products to release, in response

to a lawful authorization, either plaintext which verifiably relates to the encrypted data in question or the keys or algorithms necessary to retrieve the plaintext. Appropriate sanctions will be put in place in respect of failure to comply."

Ireland is a party to the Wassenaar Arrangement and restricts the export of cryptography as a dual-use item under both the Wassenaar Arrangement redundant and the European Union. In December 1998, Ireland subscribed to the more restrictive Wassenaar Dual-Use Control List. Irish export controls are implemented in the:

- Control of Exports Act 1983 (No. 35 of 1983);
- Control of Exports Order 1996 (SI No. 363 of 1996) (lists military and paramilitary items subject to export licensing);
- European Communities (Control of Exports of Dual-Use Goods) Regulations 1996 (SI No. 362 of 1996) (provides penalties for breaches of the 1994 EU Dual-Use Regulation);
- Customs Act 1956 (No. 7 of 1956).

The Export Licensing Unit of the Department of Enterprise, Trade and Employment is responsible for licensing exports of cryptographic products.

A letter from the Irish Development Agency dated February 21, 1994, stated that Ireland does not impose any export restrictions on computer software. The letter concluded that that was the reason that "over 75 overseas software companies" had established operations in Ireland. Some of these firms have established a large international market presence for cryptographic products. For example, the number of monthly licenses issued by the Export Licensing Unit for the export of dual civilian-military use goods, including cryptographic products, has increased to some 200. Companies, such as Baltimore Technologies, desiring to export cryptographic products must receive a license. The licenses, which list the country to which the encryption may be exported, are valid for six months. The Export Licensing Unit does not release details on the companies concerned nor the quantity or value of the encryption products being exported.

Irish Encryption Export Licenses granted in 1998 (Jan.- Oct.):

Month	Number	Destination Countries
January	6	Netherlands, Denmark, Romania,
Egypt, Brunei, Belgium		
February	5	Germany, Thailand, Finland,
Australia, Denmark		
March	9	Netherlands, Australia, Germany,
	Finland, New Zealand,	Italy
April	7	Japan, Germany, Belgium, Denmark,
	France, Egypt	
May	14	Brazil, Mexico, Netherlands,
	Australia, Denmark, Egypt	
June	10	Iceland, Andorra, Germany, Israel,
	Saudi Arabia	
July	7	China, Andorra, France, Germany,
	Italy, Qatar, USA	
August	0	
September	17	Croatia, Japan, Netherlands, Slovenia,
	South	
		Korea, Taiwan, Thailand, Germany,
	Italy, Spain	
October	24	Canada, France, Romania, USA, Japan,
	New Zealand,	
		Philippines, South Korea, UK,
	Finland	

Ref: Irish Crypto Policy <http://www.irlgov.ie/tec/html/signat.htm>
OECD Group of Experts on Information Security and Privacy, Inventory of Controls on Cryptographic Technologies (DSTI/ICCP/REG(98)4/REV3), September 23, 1998.

Israel

199 RED/YELLOW
1998 RED

Israel has comprehensive regulations regarding the export, import, and domestic use of encryption products. In July 1997, Industry and Trade Ministry Chief Scientist Orna Berry told the *Jerusalem Post* that the Israeli legal system bowed to U.S. pressure when it devised its encryption laws. Berry said "The Israeli legal system has not done a good job in considering the impact of these laws, and they have bent in front of pressure from the Americans". However, these controls do not appeared to be enforced and many of the top cryptographers and cryptoanalysts reside in Israel.

According to the NSA/Commerce report, the rules are enforced under a Court Order entitled "The Supervision On Products and Utilities (Dealing With Encryption Means), 1974, based upon the Supervision on Products and Utilities Law of 1957." The court order states persons will not engage in encryption activities, includes import, export, production or use, unless they are licensed by the Military Export and Assistance Division of the Ministry of Defense (SIBAT). Israel has been discussing loosening controls on encryption used solely for authentication purposes and adopting some of the provisions of the Wassenaar Arrangement. Industry and Trade Minister Natan Sharansky appealed to the Justice Ministry to revise the law in 1997.

State Department Tel Aviv Cable 11049-93 provides similar information. It states the "regulation of import and export of encryption devices and development of encryption technologies is handled by the Ministry of Defense, the same as the export of arms. Encryption exports must receive an export license specifying the end-user. A company wishing to develop encryption technology must first receive a license from the Ministry of Defense."

Ref: Chief scientist: Legal system gave in to U.S. pressure on patent laws, The Jerusalem Post, July 7, 1997.
A Study of the International Market for Computer Software with Encryption , U.S. Department of Commerce and the National Security Agency, July 1995.
<http://cwis.kub.nl/~frw/people/koops/cls2.htm#is>

Italy

1999 GREEN/YELLOW
1998 GREEN/YELLOW

There are no prohibitions on the import of cryptography into Italy. The Treasury may demand access to the plain text of encrypted files. The Italian Parliament has twice attempted to pass legislation requiring the deposit of encryption keys with the Ministry of Posts and Telecommunications.

On March 15, 1997, the Italian Parliament passed Law 59/97. Article 15 (2) of the law establishes framework for electronically signed documents using digital signatures. The digital signature system uses asymmetric encryption. The technical standards on the encryption keys were to be implemented under a separate law. Certificate authorities are to be licensed by the government and escrowed keys are to be held by notaries public.

Italy controls exports of cryptography pursuant to the Wassenaar Arrangement and the EU Dual-Use Regulation. In December 1998, Italy subscribed to the more restrictive Wassenaar Dual-Use Control List. The Ministry of Foreign Trade controls exports of cryptographic products. It is advised on export licenses by the Defense Ministry, Foreign Ministry, Interior Ministry, the military intelligence service (SISMI), and the civilian intelligence service (SISDE). Authority to control cryptographic exports is contained in Article 2 of Italian Law no. 89 of February 24, 1997.

There is confusion about the applicability of Italy's export laws to intangible exports of cryptographic software.

Ref: OECD Group of Experts on Information Security and Privacy, Inventory of Controls on Cryptographic Technologies (DSTI/ICCP/REG(98)4/REV3), September 23, 1998.
A Study of the International Market for Computer Software with Encryption , U.S. Department of Commerce and the National Security Agency, July 1995.

Japan

1999 GREEN/YELLOW
1998 YELLOW

According to the Ministry of International Trade and Industry (MITI) and Japan's report to the OECD, there are no domestic restrictions on the private use of cryptography in Japan. There are also no import restrictions on cryptographic equipment in Japan. The Ministry of Posts and Telecommunications is responsible for developing policy on private and commercial encryption usage on the national telecommunications network.

Japan enforces export controls on cryptography pursuant to the Wassenaar Dual-Use List. Exports are regulated by the:

- Foreign Exchange and Foreign Trade Law (Law No. 228, 1949);
- Foreign Exchange Order (Cabinet Order No. 260, 1980);
- Export Trade Control Order (Cabinet Order No. 63, 1949); and
- International Trade Administration Bureau Notification (No. 492), 1992).

The licensing authority for exports is the Security Export Control Division of the Ministry of International Trade and Industry (MITI). Export relief was granted in February 1998 for products determined to be less sensitive, including DVD and pay television devices. Export laws apply to both tangible and intangible cryptographic exports.

On 24 June 1997, Nikkei America reported that MITI initiated stricter export inspection of products incorporating cryptographic technology. MITI announced that it would inspect such items with an eye to national security issues and prevention of terrorist activities. The new policy has reduced the trading volume of computers, software and IC cards. It became necessary for exporters to get MITI permission to export products using cryptography and the inspection time has increased from a few weeks to over a month in some cases, said a spokesman for an electric machinery manufacturer. MITI started stricter inspection after the U.S. government revised its regulations in October 1997. It changed the minimum product price requiring inspection from more than 1 million yen to 50,000 yen.

Ref: OECD Group of Experts on Information Security and Privacy, Inventory of Controls on Cryptographic Technologies (DSTI/ICCP/REG(98)4/REV3), September 23, 1998.
Email correspondence with Ministry of Trade and Industry, January 1999.
A Study of the International Market for Computer Software with Encryption , U.S. Department of Commerce and the National Security Agency, July 1995.
http://www.jya.com/mitizeal.txt

Kazakhstan

1999 RED
1998 Not reported

The domestic use of cryptography is controlled by Resolution No. 967, Article 240 (13 June 1997) and Regulation No. 27. A license from the Licensing Commission of the Committee of National Security (KNB) is required for the research and development, manufacture, repair, routine maintenance, sale, and advertising of cryptographic products.

Kazakhstan controls both the import and export of cryptographic products. The applicable law is Resolution No. 1037, Article 266 (30 June 1997) and Regulation No. 29. An export license is required from the KNB. KNB decisions are subject to judicial oversight.

Ref: <http://cwis.kub.nl/~frw/people/koops/cls2.htm>

Kenya

1999 GREEN/YELLOW
1998 Not reported

Kenya reportedly maintains no export, import, or domestic use controls on cryptographic products.

On September 16, 1998, the United States authorized the export of unlimited strength encryption products (with or without key recovery) to the banking and financial, insurance, health and medical, and on-line electronic commercial sectors in Kenya. This is an indication that the U.S. has leveraged its authority to gain access to plain text information in those sectors within the country under Mutual Legal Assistance Treaty (MLAT)/Financial Action Task Force (FATF) provisions.

Ref: White House Press Announcement, September 16, 1998.

Korea, Republic of (South Korea)

1999 GREEN/YELLOW
1998 YELLOW

In its report to the OECD, the Republic of Korea stated there are neither import restrictions nor prohibitions against using cryptography in the private sector. The government is investigating a public key management regime.

The Republic of Korea restricts the export of cryptographic hardware and software pursuant to the Wassenaar Arrangement. Regulations on exports are governed by the Public Notice on Export and Import of Strategic Goods issued pursuant to the Foreign Trade Act and its accompanying Decree. The licensing authority for exports is the Ministry of Commerce, Industry, and Energy.

Ref: OECD Group of Experts on Information Security and Privacy, Inventory of Controls on Cryptographic Technologies (DSTI/ICCP/REG(98)4/REV3), September 23, 1998.

Kuwait

1999 GREEN
1998 UNKNOWN

According to the Ministry of Commerce and Industry in Kuwait, there are no export, import, or domestic use controls on cryptography in Kuwait.

Ref: Embassy of the Sate of Kuwait letter dated August 4, 1997.
E-mail, Ministry of Commerce and Industry, Kuwait, Kuwait, January 11, 1999.

Kyrgyzstan

1999 GREEN
1998 Not reported

There are no export, import, or domestic use controls on cryptography in Kyrgyzstan.

PGP and other cryptographic programs can be downloaded freely from http://www.underground.org.kg/crypto/.

Ref: <http://cwis.kub.nl/~frw/people/koops/cls2.htm>

Latvia

1999 GREEN
1998 GREEN

There are no restrictions on the import or use of cryptography in Latvia. As a candidate for membership in the EU, Latvia regulates encryption exports pursuant to the EU Dual-Use List.

NATO representatives have urged Latvia to adopt key recovery schemes as a pre-condition for joining the Western alliance. On the other hand, the EU has rejected the key recovery approach and Germany, in particular, is said to have warned Latvia that it would have to adopt the EU policy on cryptography before joining the Union.

Ref: "U.S. Assault on Northern Europe," *Intelligence Newsletter*, No. 342, September 17, 1998.

Lebanon

1999 GREEN
1998 Not reported

Lebanon does not maintain import, export, or domestic use controls on cryptography. There is no agency charged with setting policy on the issue.

Ref: E-mail, dtd. January 24, 1999 from Advisor to the General Director, Ministry of Post & Telecommunications, Lebanese Republic.

Liechtenstein

1999 GREEN

1998 GREEN

There are no restrictions on the import or use of cryptography in Liechtenstein.

Liechtenstein is a noted tax haven on the Swiss-Austrian border. It is neither a member of the European Union nor the Wassenaar Arrangement. Significantly, it was not on the list of countries eligible to receive U.S. general purpose encryption commodities and software under a U.S. Commerce Department license exception. This indicates that there are mutual legal assistance difficulties between the U.S. and Liechtenstein. The country maintains strict confidentiality controls on banking and company information held by its firms. Although it did not respond to the letter sent to its U.N. Mission, its banking laws may yield a clue on its feeling on third-party encryption holders. According to its laws, Liechtenstein authorities will not assist third party inquiries relating to foreign tax obligations.

Ref: White House Press Announcement, September 16, 1998.

Lithuania

1999 GREEN
1998 GREEN

According to the Embassy of Lithuania in Washington, there are no laws in Lithuania governing the use, export, or import of cryptography. The Lithuanian Parliament network was also queried for information for any proposed legislation. The results were negative. The Embassy informed us that the policies on the use of cryptography in Lithuania would normally come under the jurisdiction of the Ministry of Communications and Informatics in Vilnius. The Department of Export-Import Regulation of Ministry of Economy is in charge of export controls.

NATO representatives have urged Lithuania to adopt key recovery schemes as a pre-condition for joining the Western alliance. However, the EU has rejected the key recovery approach and Germany, in particular, is said to told Lithuania that it would have to adopt the EU policy on cryptography before joining the Union.

Ref: Embassy of the Republic of Lithuania fax dated June 30, 1997.
"U.S. Assault on Northern Europe," *Intelligence Newsletter*, No. 342, September 17, 1998.

Luxembourg

1999 GREEN/YELLOW
1998 GREEN/YELLOW

There are no domestic controls or import restrictions on cryptography in Luxembourg.

Luxembourg controls the export of cryptographic items pursuant to the Wassenaar Arrangement, of which it is a participant, and the EU Dual-Use Regulation.

Ref: OECD Group of Experts on Information Security and Privacy, Inventory of Controls on Cryptographic Technologies (DSTI/ICCP/REG(98)4/REV3), September 23, 1998.

Malaysia

1999 YELLOW
1998 YELLOW

There are no export, import or domestic use controls on cryptography in Malaysia.

However, in May 1997, the Malaysian parliament passed a law on digital signatures that provides a framework of legal certainty for electronic transactions. The law provides for key verification and deposit of public keys with trusted third parties. The government licenses the trusted third parties. The law does not specify the technical details for the key escrow system.

In July 1998, the Dewan Rakyat (House of Representatives) approved the Communications and Multimedia Bill, which has several sections on telecommunications privacy. Section 234 prohibits unlawful interception of communications. Section 249 sets rules for searches of computers and includes access to encryption keys. Section 252 authorizes police to intercept communications without a warrant if a public prosecutor considers that a communication is likely to contain information which is relevant to an investigation.

Ref: Communications and Multimedia Bill 1998
<http://www.kttp.gov.my/mm/multimedia.htm>.
http://www2.echo.lu /legal/en/news/9709/capter7.html#2
http://www.geocities.com /Tokyo/9239/digisign.htm l

Mexico

1999 GREEN
1998 GREEN

Mexico reported to the OECD that there are no domestic controls on the use of encryption in Mexico. It also claimed that there are no export or import restrictions on encryption technology.

Ref: Inventory of Controls on Cryptography Technologies, Group of Experts on Information Security and Privacy, Organization for Economic Cooperation and Development (DSTI/ICCP/REG(98)4/REV3), 23 September 1998.

Monaco

1999 GREEN
1998 Not reported

There are no prohibitions on the use of hardware or software cryptographic products in Monaco. No agency controls the use of the technology.

According to Monaco Telematique, a Monaco Internet services company, Monaco does not have any export controls on cryptography. However, Monaco has a trade agreement with France and, therefore, French customs regulations apply to the principality. If a Monegasque company wanted to export a hardware encryption device, French customs might attempt to block the export. However, no restrictions are placed on the export of intangible encryption software from the principality.

There are similarly no import restrictions on cryptography. However, French customs could hinder the passage of strong encryption devices to Monaco, since on occasion they check parcels going to Monaco. There are no restrictions on the import of intangible software encryption to the principality.

On September 16, 1998, the United States authorized the export of unlimited strength encryption products (with or without key recovery) to the banking and financial, insurance, health and medical, and on-line electronic commercial sectors in Monaco. This is an indication that the U.S. has leveraged its authority to gain access to plain text information in those sectors within the country under Mutual Legal Assistance Treaty (MLAT)/Financial Action Task Force (FATF) provisions.

Ref: E-Mail, Monaco Telematique MC-TEL, January 9, 1999.
White House Press Announcement, September 16, 1998.

Mongolia

1999 RED
1998 Not reported

According to the Defense Attache of the Mongolian Embassy in Washington, there are no export controls on cryptographic products in Mongolia since the country does not produce or otherwise manufacture such technology. There are import controls and domestic use controls on cryptography. Cryptography may only be used by lawful enterprises approved by the National Security Board.

Ref: E-mail, Defense Attache of the Mongolian Embassy, Washington, January 27, 1999.

Morocco

1999 GREEN
1998 Not reported

There are reportedly no domestic use controls, export, or import controls on cryptography in Morocco.

Mount Athos, Republic of

1999 GREEN
1998 GREEN

The Holy Mount is a self-governed part of the Greek state subject to the Ministry of Foreign Affairs in its political affairs. It is a Greek Orthodox Vatican City without the diplomatic recognition and without the same degree of independence.

It has taken a strong stance against pan-European law enforcement measures and agreements. The monks who live in this monastic republic are strongly committed to personal privacy. The republic's unique status could make it a cryptographic safe haven in Europe. On June 5, 1997, representatives from 20 monasteries of Mount Athos held an meeting to express their views prior to the Greek Parliament's ratification of the pan-European Schengen Agreement on law enforcement. If Athens attempted to implement the agreement, the monks stressed, the state would find itself up against all of Mount Athos' monks "as conscientious objectors."

Ref: Athens News Agency Bulletin (No 1202), June 3, 1997.
http://www-media.dbnet.ece. ntua.gr/Athos.html

Myanmar (Burma)

1999 RED
1998 Not reported

Myanmar bans the use of cryptography except that used for official government and armed forces (Tatmadaw) communications. Because several insurgent opposition groups use encryption illegally, possession of such technology can result in long imprisonment or execution. A few rebel groups use strong encryption, thus foiling the attempts by Burmese cryptanalysts to decode communications and stored data. However, some rebels use poor encryption, especially that used for field communications.

Ref: Desmond Ball, "SIGINT strengths form a vital part of Burma's military muscle," *Jane's Intelligence Review*, Vol. 10, No. 3, March 1, 1998.

Nauru

1999 GREEN
1998 GREEN

According to the Honorary Counsel of Nauru in the United Kingdom, there are no applicable laws in Nauru governing the use, import, or export of cryptography. The responsible office for determining any such future policies is the Secretariat for External Affairs in Nauru. Nauru is an independent island in the central Pacific that is eight square miles with a population of 8,000.

Ref: Republic of Nauru Honorary Counsel, Sevenoaks, UK fax dated June 27, 1997.

Netherlands

1999 GREEN/YELLOW
1998 GREEN/YELLOW

There are no restrictions on the domestic use of cryptography in the Netherlands, including that used for public and private radio systems. In

March 1994, the Netherlands government advanced a draft parliamentary bill that would have prohibited the possession, use, and marketing of powerful encryption products without a license. After a national outcry, the bill was withdrawn.

[Computer II Bill]

The Netherlands applies export controls on cryptographic hardware and software in accordance with the Wassenaar Arrangement and the European Union Dual-Use Regulation. It also supported the changes to the Wassenaar control list announced in December 1998. The export of cryptographic equipment from the Netherlands requires an individual license for all nations except Belgium and Luxembourg. The applicable statutes are the 1962 Law on Import and Export (Dutch Statute Book 1962, 295) and the ministerial Decree on Export of Strategic Goods and its Annex (Dutch Statute Book 1963, 128).

The licensing authority for exports is the Central Agency of Import and Export, a component of the Ministry of Economic Affairs. The National Communications Security Agency (NCSA) has the responsibility for determining the impact that specific exports of cryptographic equipment may have on national security. The Commerce/NSA report heavily redacts further information on the activities of the NCSA, although it is known that this agency performs many of the functions of the NSA. Dutch export law only applies to tangible products, not intangible software transmitted electronically.

There are no import controls on cryptography.

Ref: Email Communication from Directorate-General for Telecommunications and Post, Feb. 10, 1999.
Inventory of Controls on Cryptography Technologies, Group of Experts on Information Security and Privacy, Organization for Economic Cooperation and Development (DSTI/ICCP/REG(98)4/REV3), 23 September 1998.
A Study of the International Market for Computer Software with Encryption , U.S. Department of Commerce and the National Security Agency, July 1995.
http://www.db.nl/english/Legal.html

Netherlands Antilles

1999 GREEN/YELLOW
1998 GREEN/YELLOW

The Cabinet Minister for the Netherlands Antilles in s'Gravenhage, the Netherlands informed us that the Department of Justice of the Netherlands Antilles located in Willemstad, Curaçao had responsibility for establishing a policy on the use of cryptography.

Significantly, the Netherlands Antilles was not on the list of countries eligible to receive U.S. general purpose encryption commodities and software under a U.S. Commerce Department license exception, while the neighboring island of Aruba was granted such an exception. This indicates that there are mutual legal assistance difficulties between the U.S. and the Netherlands Antilles.

Ref: Het Kabinet Van De Gevolmachtigde Minister Van De Nederlandse Antillen fax dated June 30, 1997.
White House Press Announcement, September 16, 1998.

New Zealand

1999 GREEN/YELLOW
1998 GREEN/YELLOW

There are no import or domestic use controls on cryptography.

New Zealand maintains export controls on cryptography pursuant to its participation in the Wassenaar Arrangement. It adhered to the changes to the Wassenaar Control List announced in December 1998. Applicable export laws are the Customs and Excise Act 1996 and the Customs Prohibition Order 1996. The Customs and Excise Act's Section 54, "Prohibited Exports," states that "The Governor-General may from time to time, by Order in Council, prohibit the exportation from New Zealand of any specified goods or goods of a specified class or classes" (followed by a list of specific conditions on prohibitions). Cryptographic exports require a strategic export permit issued by the International Security & Arms Control Division of the Ministry of Foreign Affairs and Trade (MFAT). The Government Communications Security Bureau (GCSB), the New Zealand equivalent of the NSA, advises MFAT on approving exports of cryptography. Only tangible exports of cryptography are covered except when intangible exports contribute to a weapon of mass destruction program.

According to the MFAT, permits are based on the following factors:

- end user of the product
- country of destination for the export
- nature of the goods
- documentary evidence of the *bona fides* of the end user.

The New Zealand government relies on the United States government's export policies as a guideline for acceptability. According to the MFAT, no formal licenses have been denied, although some license requests have been informally discouraged.

Ref: Fax message from NZ Ministry of Foreign Affairs and Trade, January 1999.
Inventory of Controls on Cryptography Technologies, Group of Experts on Information Security and Privacy, Organization for Economic Cooperation and Development (DSTI/ICCP/REG(98)4/REV3), 23 September 1998.
A Study of the International Market for Computer Software with Encryption , U.S. Department of Commerce and the National Security Agency, July 1995.
http://www.cs.auckland.ac.nz/~pgut001/policy/

Nicaragua

1999 UNKNOWN
1998 UNKNOWN

During our first survey, we were informed that the Center for Exports and Imports (CEI) in Managua, Nicaragua was responsible for cryptography exports and imports in Nicaragua. Follow-up correspondence with that agency yielded no further information.

Ref: Phone call from CEI, Managua, Nicaragua, December 1997.

Niue

1999 GREEN
1998 Not reported

Niue is a self-governing territory of New Zealand in the South Pacific. It maintains no export controls, import controls, or domestic use controls on encryption. The Telecommunications Minister reports that "people may bring whatever encryption devices they wish." No government agency is charged with regulating cryptography.

Ref: E-mail dtd. January 25, 1999 from Hon. Terry Coe, Minister of Telecommunications, Government of Niue.

Norfolk Island

1999 GREEN
1998 GREEN

Norfolk Island is a self-governing territory under the authority of Australia. It is not part of Australia. It is located in the Tasman Sea east of Australia.

According to Norfolk Island Data Services, there are no references in Norfolk Island's Telecommunications Act to restrictions placed on encryption programs transmitted to and from the island.

Ref: http://www.names.nf
E-mail dated January 21, 1999, Norfolk Island Data Services, 909 Fletcher Christian Road, Norfolk Island, South Pacific.

Norway

1999 GREEN/YELLOW

1998 GREEN

There are no domestic use prohibitions nor are there import controls in Norway.

Norway controls the export of cryptographic products pursuant to its participation in the Wassenaar Arrangement. Norway adheres to the revised Wassenaar Control List announced in December 1998. Exports are controlled by the:

- Act of December 18, 1987 (Royal Decree No. 93) related to the Export Control of Strategic Goods, Services, Technologies, etc.;
- Regulations of January 10, 1989 for the Implementation of the Export Control of Strategic Goods, Services, Technologies, etc.

The administering authority for cryptographic export licensing is the Section for Export and Import Controls of the Ministry of Foreign Affairs. Norway previously applied the General Software Note exemption of Wassenaar to Internet distributions of cryptography.

Ref: Inventory of Controls on Cryptography Technologies, Group of Experts on Information Security and Privacy, Organization for Economic Cooperation and Development (DSTI/ICCP/REG(98)4/REV3), 23 September 1998.
A Study of the International Market for Computer Software with Encryption , U.S. Department of Commerce and the National Security Agency, July 1995.

Pakistan

1999 RED
1998 RED

All encryption hardware and software must be inspected and authorized by the Pakistan Telecommunications Authority (PTA) before sale and use. Algorithms and keys must be inspected and deposited with the PTA. The governing law is the Pakistan Telecommunication (Reorganization) Act. Pakistan also severely restricts the use of voice encryption used in cellular networks.

Ref: http://cwis.kub.nl/~frw/people/koops/cls2.htm#pa

Palestine

1999 UNKNOWN
1998 Not reported

The Palestinian Ministry of Information informed us that the Palestinian Ministry of Telecommunications was responsible for setting policy on the use of encryption in Palestine. No further information was forthcoming from that agency.

Ref: E-Mail, Palestinian Ministry of Information, February 1, 1999.

Papua New Guinea

1999 GREEN
1998 GREEN

The Embassy of Papua New Guinea in Washington informed us that they were not aware of any laws in their country concerning cryptography. However, they informed us that jurisdiction for the technology was under the purview of the Department of the Attorney General.

Ref: Embassy of Papua New Guinea letter dated August 19, 1997.

Philippines

1999 GREEN
1998 GREEN

The use of cryptographic hardware and software is not currently controlled in the Philippines.

Pitcairn Islands

1999 GREEN
1998 Not reported

According to the Commissioner of the Pitcairn Islands, there are no import, export or domestic use controls on computer or phone encryption in the British territory. One minor exception is that the Amateur Radio Service prohibits voice scrambling and data encryption, in accordance with international radio regulations.

If an encryption policy were needed in the future, it would be considered by the Pitcairn Islands Administration in consultation with the Pitcairn Island Council and the U.K. Foreign and Commonwealth Office.

Ref: E-Mail, dtd. January 25, 1999, Hon. Leon Salt, Commissioner for the Pitcairn Islands.

Poland

1999 GREEN/YELLOW
1998 GREEN/YELLOW

There are no restrictions on the domestic use of cryptography in Poland.

Poland implements export controls on cryptography pursuant to its participation in the Wassenaar Arrangement. Poland supported the changes to the Wassenaar Control List announced in December 1998. Export licenses must be obtained from the Export Control Department of the Ministry of Foreign Trade. Encryption software is evaluated on a case-by-case basis.

Imports of cryptography require either a general authorization or an import certificate. The Ministry of Foreign Trade coordinates imports with the U.S. Bureau of Export Administration (BXA) including determining whether or not to issue import permits.

Ref: Inventory of Controls on Cryptography Technologies, Group of Experts on Information Security and Privacy, Organization for Economic Cooperation and Development (DSTI/ICCP/REG(98)4/REV3), 23 September 1998.
"Poland- Networking Hardware & Software Market," U.S. & Foreign Commercial Service and U.S. Department of State, July 1998.
A Study of the International Market for Computer Software with Encryption , U.S. Department of Commerce and the National Security Agency, July 1995.

Portugal

1999 GREEN/YELLOW
1998 GREEN/YELLOW

There are no controls on the import of cryptography or its domestic use.

Portugal regulates the export of encryption in accordance with its participation in the Wassenaar Arrangement and its implementation of the EU Dual-Use Regulation. According to Portugal's report to the OECD, the licensing authority is the Directorate-General for Commerce.

Ref: Inventory of Controls on Cryptography Technologies, Group of Experts on Information Security and Privacy, Organization for Economic Cooperation and Development (DSTI/ICCP/REG(98)4/REV3), 23 September 1998.

Romania

1999 GREEN/YELLOW
1998 GREEN/YELLOW

There are no import or domestic use controls on cryptography in Romania.

Romania regulates the export of encryption pursuant to its participation in the Wassenaar Arrangement. The licensing authority is the Department of Foreign Trade of the Ministry of Commerce.

Ref: http://cwis.kub.nl/~frw/people/koops/cls2.htm#ro

Russia

1999 RED
1998 RED

The import of cryptography and its domestic use is regulated in Russia by the following:

- Section 5 of Edict Number 334, of April 3, 1995, issued by the President of Russia, prohibits the import of cryptographic products without a license.
- Section 4 of Edict Number 334, of April 3, 1995, issued by the President of Russia, prohibits all activities in the development, sale, and use of cryptography without a license issued by the Federal Agency for Government Communications and Information (FAPSI), Russia's equivalent of the NSA.
- Joint Decision No. 60 of the State Technical Committee and FAPSI of June 24, 1997 set forth procedures for obtaining import and domestic use licenses for cryptography.

Russia is a participant in the Wassenaar Arrangement and restricts the export of cryptographic hardware and software. It adheres to the Wassenaar Dual-Use Control List announced in December 1998.

According to the Commerce NSA report, upon the disintegration of the U.S.S.R., the President of Russia issued five decrees:

- Decree No. 179 of February 22, 1992
- Decree No. 312 of March 27, 1992
- Decree No. 388 of April 11, 1992
- Decree No. 469 of May 12, 1992
- Decree No. 507 of July 5, 1992

These decrees along with the Law on Defense Industry Conversion, laid down certain legal foundations for a national armaments and military technologies control system.

The decrees were consolidated in 1994 by the Statute on Controls of Exports from the Russian Federation of Certain Types of Raw and Processed Materials, Equipment, Technology, Scientific and Technical Information Which Can Be Used in the Production of Weapons or Military Equipment as ratified by the President of the Russian Federation under Decree 74 dated February 11, 1994. Included in this statute is a list of commodities, which require an individually approved license, issued by the Ministry of Foreign Economic Relations, for export from Russia. Cryptographic equipment and software (including mass-market) is identified in the list of commodities requiring individually approved export licenses.

The laws apply to both tangible and intangible cryptographic products.

Ref: A Study of the International Market for Computer Software with Encryption , U.S. Department of Commerce and the National Security Agency, July 1995.

Saudi Arabia

1999 YELLOW/RED
1998 GREEN

It is reported that Saudi Arabia prohibits the domestic use of encryption. According to the NIST survey, Saudi Arabia has neither import nor export controls on cryptography in effect.

Ref: NIST Preliminary Results of Study of Non - U.S. Cryptography Laws/Regulations, September 27, 1993.
http://cwis.kub.nl/~frw/people/koops/cls2.htm

Singapore

1999 RED
1998 RED

According to the Singapore Trade Development Board, "there are no domestic restrictions on the use of cryptography software and hardware, except that hardware equipment that will be connected directly to the telecommunications infrastructure will require approval from the Telecommunication Authority (TA) of Singapore. This is to ensure compliance and non-interference with telecommunications requirements."

In 1998, Singapore enacted the Electronic Transactions Act. Regulations were released by the National Computer Board in February 1999. The regulations describe it as "a voluntary licensing scheme for certification authorities (CAs)"

There are both import and export controls on encryption products. According the to TDB:

> In Singapore, imports and exports on all physical goods and products require permits issued by the Trade Development Board (TDB) of Singapore. TDB is the administrative agency responsible for imports and exports in Singapore.
>
> For the import of cryptographic products, an additional application form containing the technical specifications, purpose and end-user of the product needs to be completed. The import of the product is generally granted, especially if the product is for use within a company. Automatic approval is given for certain classes of mass-use products.
>
> For exports of cryptographic products, TDB also requires a permit in the same way as other products. However, no separate application form is needed. For re-exports of cryptographic products from other countries, they will be subject to the agreement or laws of the originating country.

Singapore is a major supplier of encryption products to Myanmar.

Ref: Singapore Trade Development Board fax dated January 23, 1999.
Singapore Trade Development Board fax dated August 11, 1997.

Electronic Transactions Act, 1998. < http://www.cca.gov.sg/eta/index.html>
Desmond Ball, "SIGINT strengths form a vital part of Burma's military muscle," *Jane's Intelligence Review*, Vol. 10, No. 3, March 1, 1998.

Slovakia

1999 YELLOW
1998 GREEN/YELLOW

There are no domestic use controls of cryptography in Slovakia.

Slovakia regulates the export of cryptography pursuant to its participation in the Wassenaar Agreement. Slovakia adhered to the revised Wassenaar Dual-Use Control List announced in December 1998. The licensing authority is the Ministry of Economy.

Slovakia also regulates the import of cryptography. Import licenses are issued by the Ministry of Economy.

Ref: http://www.wassenaar.org
http://cwis.kub.nl/~frw/people/koops/cls2.htm

Slovenia

1999 GREEN
1998 GREEN

There are no export, import, or domestic use prohibitions on cryptography. Significantly, Slovenia, unlike neighboring Croatia, was not on the list of countries eligible to receive U.S. general purpose encryption commodities and software under a U.S. Commerce Department license exception. This indicates that there are mutual legal assistance difficulties between the U.S. and Slovenia.

Ref: http://cwis.kub.nl/~frw/people/koops/cls2.htm

South Africa

1999 GREEN/YELLOW
1998 YELLOW

There are no domestic controls on the use of encryption in South Africa. There are many companies in SA active in the development of crypto products.

According to the Commerce/NSA report, the South African government controls encryption exports and imports as a dual-use item on the General Armaments Control Schedule. Exports of encryption require an individual validated license. The control of encryption is under the jurisdiction of the South African Department of Defense Armaments Development and Protection Act, 1968, No. R. 888, published on May 13, 1994.

An individual validated license was previously required for the import of encryption software. A valid permit from the Armaments Control Division is required for the import or transportation of cryptographic equipment or software. This information is gleaned from State Department Johannesburg Cable 000951, June 23, 1995.

The South African Telecommunications Regulation Authority (SATRA) regulates the use of encryption over telecommunications facilities but not for internal computer systems.

Ref: A Study of the International Market for Computer Software with Encryption , U.S. Department of Commerce and the National Security Agency, July 1995.

Spain

1999 YELLOW
1998 YELLOW

There are no domestic controls on encryption. However, on April 8th 1998, the Spanish Congress approved the *Ley General de Telecomunicaciones*

(Telecommunications General Law). The law includes article 52, which could provide a basis for establishment of a key-recovery regime. Article 52 (2) states:

> "Among their conditions of use, when it (encryption) is used to protect the confidentiality of information, an obligation could be imposed to notify either a General Administration body, or a public organisation about the algorithm or whatever encryption procedure is used, with an effect to control it following prevailing normatives. This obligation will affect all the developers which incorporate cryptography in their equipments or devices, the operators that include it in their networks or in the services they offer, and, if applicable, to the users that employ it"

Spain regulates the exports of cryptography pursuant to its participation in the Wassenaar Arrangement. It supported the decision of the group to amend the Dual-Use Control List in December 1998. The governing law is Royal Decree 491/1998 of March 27, 1998, Regulating the Foreign Trade of Defense Materials and Dual-Use Items. The law implements both the Wassenaar Arrangement and the EU Dual-Use Regulation. The licensing authority is an Inter-ministerial Committee (*Junta Interministerial Reguladora del Comercio de Material de Defensa y Doble Uso [JIMDDU]*) charged with regulating the export of cryptographic items. The committee is presided over by the Secretary General for Commerce and includes representatives of the Defense, Foreign Affairs, and Economic Ministries. Licenses are approved or denied on an individual basis dependent upon the effects on Spanish foreign policy or national defense as well as international commitments. Advice is provided to the committee by the National Cryptologic Center of the *Centro Superior de Informacion de la Defensa* (CESID), the Spanish intelligence service. The export law applies to both tangible and intangible exports of software.

There are no import prohibitions on cryptography.

Ref: Ministry of Planning, Madrid fax dated July 21, 1997.
LEY 11/1998, de 24 de abril, General de Telecomunicaciones.
<http://www.asertel.es/cs/08017002.htm>.
http://www.gilc.org/crypto/spain/gilc-crypto-spain-798.html

A Study of the International Market for Computer Software with Encryption , U.S. Department of Commerce and the National Security Agency, July 1995.
Inventory of Controls on Cryptography Technologies, Group of Experts on Information Security and Privacy, Organization for Economic Cooperation and Development (DSTI/ICCP/REG(98)4/REV3), 23 September 1998.

Sri Lanka

1999 GREEN
1998 Not reported

Sri Lanka maintains no import, export, or domestic use prohibitions on cryptography.

Ref: Email communication with Telecommunications Ministry, Feb 1999.

Swaziland

1999 GREEN
1998 GREEN

According to the Embassy of Swaziland in Washington, the country does not have policies on the importation, exportation, or domestic uses of cryptographic hardware or software.

Ref: Embassy of the Kingdom of Swaziland letter dated August 6, 1997.

Sweden

1999 GREEN/YELLOW
1998 GREEN

According to the Embassy of Sweden in Washington there are in Sweden:

- No controls on the domestic use of cryptography.

- No controls on the import of computer programs or equipment that permit cryptography.

The Swedish Cabinet Office issued a report in October 1997 titled "Cryptography Policy: Possible Courses of Action for Sweden." The report recommends that there be no domestic use prohibitions on encryption use in Sweden or any imposition of import controls. It does suggest that export controls should remain. It also offers the possibility that Swedish key deposition facilities might be created and that law enforcement should have access to keys deposited in such facilities and to those that are not.

Sweden maintains export controls on encryption pursuant to the Wassenaar Arrangement and the EU Dual-Use Regulation. Export controls are governed by the Strategic Products Act (1991:341) and the Ordinance Relating to Strategic Products (1994:2060). The licensing authority is the Inspectorate for Strategic Products (ISP), a component of the Ministry of Foreign Affairs.

Ref: Embassy of Sweden letter dated July 22, 1997.
Inventory of Controls on Cryptography Technologies, Group of Experts on Information Security and Privacy, Organization for Economic Cooperation and Development (DSTI/ICCP/REG(98)4/REV3), 23 September 1998.

Switzerland

1999 GREEN
1998 GREEN

The Embassy of Switzerland in Washington responded in some detail on its cryptographic policies. This information was supplemented by further details from the Swiss government in Bern.

1) Controls on the use of encryption software or hardware

According to the Federal Law on Telecommunications (*Loi fédérale du 21 juin 1991 sur les télécommunications*, RS 784.10) and its implementing ordinances :

- The development and manufacturing of cryptographic software and hardware is not subject to any limitation.
- The use of cryptographic software is not subject to any limitation. Ordinary licensing or notification prescriptions may apply for a range of telecommunications services.
- Cryptographic products as well as other telecommunications equipment that can be connected to a public telecommunications network must follow the basic technical requirements laid down by the Federal Council. This can be done by a declaration of conformity issued by the manufacturer or by a review by the Federal Office for Communications (FOC).

2) Controls on the import of encryption

The ordinance concerning the Export, Import, and Transit of Dual-Use Goods and Specific Military Goods from June 25 1997 does not stipulate any licensing obligation for the import of products, including cryptographic hardware and software.

The only rules applicable in this context are those relating to the Import Certificate (IC). The IC is one of the documents that may be necessary for the supplier to obtain an export license from the authorities in the country of origin. Therefore, it is up to the authorities of the country of origin to determine whether or not an IC is required from the country of destination in order to get a license.

- For imports of cryptographic equipment, Switzerland issues an IC only if there is a formal request from the country of origin.
- As for exports of cryptographic equipment, Switzerland normally requires the presentation of an IC from all the countries of end-use whose authorities issue such a document. Member countries of all the four international export control regimes (The Australia Group (AG), the Missile Technology Control Regime (MTCR), the Nuclear Supplier's Group (NSG), and the Wassenaar Arrangement (WA)) are exempted from this requirement.

3) Export controls on encryption

Encryption equipment, software, and technology are controlled under the Ordinance concerning the Export, Import, and Transit of Dual-Use Goods and Specific Military Goods from June 25, 1997 and its annexes (the International Munitions Control List and the International Industrial Control List of the Wassenaar Arrangement are included in them). Those lists are reviewed annually. Switzerland adheres to the changes in the Wassenaar Dual-Use Control List announced in December 1998 but noted that "the upcoming minor changes to Switzerland's export controls on cryptographic goods as a result of the December changes to Wassenaar will not alter the liberal Swiss Cryptography Policy...Switzerland will keep its efficient export permit process for cryptographic goods in order to encourage Swiss exports to increase their sales and share worldwide while being mindful of national security interests."

The export and re-export of cryptographic hardware, software, and technology listed in the above mentioned ordinance requires an individual validated license. However, exports to end-users in the countries which are members of all the four international export control regimes (23 countries in all) are granted under an ordinary general license (OGL).

The Swiss Federal Office for Foreign Economic Affairs (FOFEA) is the licensing agency. The specific criteria considered in determining whether to grant a license are those of Wassenaar, namely "to prevent the acquisition of armaments and sensitive dual-use items for military end-uses if the situation in a region or the behavior of a State is, or becomes, a serious concern for the participating States."

The transit is subject to a limited prohibition. If the country of origin restricts the export of the products listed in the annex (e.g., cryptographic products), their transit is forbidden if it cannot be proven (e.g., with a license) that the transfer to the country of destination is in accordance with the legislation of the country of origin. The law covers intangible exports of goods such as web-based transfers.

4) Control Authority

Export controls are overseen by the FOFEA. Restrictions on the domestic use of cryptography on public telecommunications networks are the responsibility of the FOC.

Ref: Embassy of Switzerland letter dated January 27, 1999.

Embassy of Switzerland letter dated June 31, 1997.
A Study of the International Market for Computer Software with Encryption , U.S. Department of Commerce and the National Security Agency, July 1995.

Republic of China (Taiwan)

1999 GREEN/YELLOW
1998 YELLOW

According to the Taipei Economic and Cultural Representative Office in the United States (Taiwan's de facto embassy), There is a voluntary license system for Certificate Authorities. However, it also says without defining that "the domestic use of [encryption software and hardware] should comply with applicable regulations, as set forth in the Copyright Law and Telecommunication Act."

The Republic of China's Research, Development, and Evaluation Commission of the Executive Yuan completed a report on the "Establishment of a Public Key Infrastructure" in Taiwan in November 1998. The PKI initiative states that any "Public or Private organization that wished to act as a Certificate Authority (CA) may apply or receive a license from the designated agency". The responsible agencies may be the Ministry of Economic Affairs or the Ministry of Telecommunications and Transportation. The policy "does not take into account "key escrow and recovery". Previously, the policy was described as, "After taking into consideration the needs of national security, economic development, law enforcement, and personal privacy, a feasible 'key escrow and recovery' scheme should be devised on the basis of experience gained in Europe and America."

There are no import restrictions.

Taiwan is a "cooperating" party to the Wassenaar Arrangement and controls the export of cryptography. According to the Economic Office, after November 1, 1998, the ROC's High-Tech Commodity List was modified to incorporate the Wassenaar Arrangement on Export Controls. The export of encryption software and hardware should comply with the relevant provisions in the Regulations Governing Export of High Tech Commodities issued by the Ministry of Economic Affairs. Meanwhile, if the encryption software falls within the products listed in public notice No. 07464 of Exports of Products Related to Computer Programs by the Board of Foreign Trade, MOEA issued on July 13, 1998, then it is necessary to comply with the guidelines for the Export of Products Related to Computer Programs.

Ref: Taipei Economic and Cultural Representative Office, Washington, DC letter dated February 9, 1999.
Taipei Economic and Cultural Representative Office, Washington, DC letter dated September 23, 1997.
A Study of the International Market for Computer Software with Encryption , U.S. Department of Commerce and the National Security Agency, July 1995.

Tanzania

1999 GREEN
1998 Not reported

There are reportedly no controls on the export, import, and domestic use of cryptography in Tanzania.

Tatarstan

1999 UNKNOWN
1998 Not reported

Tatarstan is an autonomous republic within the Russian Federation. It maintains an economic system and telecommunications infrastructure separate from that of Russia. We were informed by the Permanent Representative of Tatarstan in the United States that the Ministry of Economy is responsible for issues dealing with cryptography. No response was received from that agency.

Ref: E-mail, Permanent Representative of the Republic of Tatarstan in the United States, January 13, 1999.

Tonga

1999 GREEN
1998 Not reported

The Kingdom of Tonga in the South Pacific hosts a server that freely distributes over the Internet BSAFEeay, a free, public domain implementation of RSA Data Security's BSAFE Applications Programming Interface (API). The site advertises that its cryptographic offerings are "made outside the US, so there [are] no ITAR restrictions."

Ref: https://www.cypherpunks.to/

Tunisia

1999 RED
1998 Not reported

According to Decree No. 97-501 of March 14, 1997, Tunisian value-added telecommunications service providers must first obtain authorization to encrypt communications. Encryption keys must be deposited with the government. The Ministry of Communications may, in certain cases and in the interests of national security and public safety, partially or totally revoke authorizations granted to value-added telecommunications services to encrypt communications.

Ref: Official Journal of the Tunisian Republic, September 25, 1997.

Turkey

1999 GREEN/YELLOW
1998 YELLOW

There are no import or domestic controls on cryptography in Turkey.

Turkey restricts the export of cryptography pursuant to its participation in the Wassenaar Arrangement. Exports must be registered in accordance with Article 3a of the Export Regime Decree No. 95/7623 of December 22, 1995. The governing authority is the Undersecretariat for Foreign Trade (UFT). Cryptographic products for export must be registered with the Istanbul Metals and Minerals Exporters' Association (IMMIB), which assigns a registration on the applicable customs declaration. Law No. 3763 of 1940 regarding the "Control of Private Industrial Enterprises Producing War Weapons, Vehicles, Equipment, and Ammunition" requires a permit from the Ministry of National Defense for the export of cryptographic products having military purposes. The export laws only apply to tangible software.

Ref: Inventory of Controls on Cryptography Technologies, Group of Experts on Information Security and Privacy, Organization for Economic Cooperation and Development (DSTI/ICCP/REG(98)4/REV3), 23 September 1998.

Uganda

1999 GREEN
1998 Not reported

There are reportedly no controls on the export, import, or domestic use of cryptography in Uganda.

Ukraine

1999 GREEN/YELLOW
1998 YELLOW

There are no specific laws prohibiting the import or use of encryption in the Ukraine. However, a recent government edict requires that networks connecting to foreign networks be routed through government-approved centers.

Ukraine regulates the export of cryptography pursuant to its participation in the Wassenaar Agreement. Ukraine adheres to the revised Wassenaar Dual-Use Control List announced in December 1998. The export licensing authority in Ukraine is the State Export Control Service.

United Arab Emirates

1999 GREEN
1998 Not reported

There are reportedly no export, import, or domestic use prohibitions on cryptography in the United Arab Emirates.

United Kingdom

1999 YELLOW
1998 GREEN/YELLOW

There are currently neither domestic use restrictions nor are there any import controls on encryption products in the United Kingdom.

The UK has been the strongest supporter of the US's efforts to promote key escrow and limitations on encryption. The government began a Public Consultation on the regulation of Trusted Third Parties (TTPs) for the provision of encryption services in 1996 and released a Public Consultation Paper on detailed proposals for legislation on the Licensing of TTPs for the provision of encryption services in March 1997. In April 1998, the Department of Trade and Industry released a "Secure Electronic Commerce Statement" which sets out the details of the government proposal:

> We therefore intend to introduce legislation to license those bodies providing, or facilitating the provision of cryptography services. Principally these will be Trusted Third Parties, Certification Authorities and Key Recovery Agents. Such licensing arrangements will be voluntary, as business has requested, although we would hope that organisations providing services to the public will see the benefit

> of adhering to a high standard, and the public confidence that this will bring.
>
> Organisations facilitating encryption services (for example through offering key recovery or providing key management services for confidentiality) will also be encouraged to seek licences.
>
> Licensed service providers that provide encryption services will, therefore, be required to make recovery of keys (or other information protecting the secrecy of the information) possible through suitable storage arrangements.
>
> The Government intends to introduce legislation to enable law enforcement agencies to obtain a warrant for lawful access to information necessary to decrypt the content of communications or stored data.

In December 1998, the Queen Elizabeth II announced that a Secure Electronic Commerce Bill would be introduced in 1999. The bill should be introduced in the summer of 1999.

In March 1999, Prime Minister Tony Blair met with industry representatives and announced that the government was backing away from support for the linking of licensing with escrow requirements. A task force of industry and government will examine alternatives to assist law enforcement. Blair suggested that escrow might be adopted if alternatives were not sufficient.

The United Kingdom maintains export controls on cryptography pursuant to its participation in the Wassenaar Arrangement and adherence to the EU Dual-Use Control List. The United Kingdom strongly supported the amendment to the Wassenaar Dual-Use Control List announced in December 1998. Export controls are implemented under the Export of Goods (Control) Order 1994 as amended by the Dual-Use and Related Goods (Export Control) Regulations 1996. The licensing authority is the Export Control Department of the Department of Trade and Industry (DTI). It has recently taken steps, spelled out in a Strategic Export Controls White Paper, to extend export controls beyond tangible cryptography to intangible exports of encryption programs over the Internet.

According to the Department of Trade and Industry (DTI), "an export license may be obtained by applying to the DTI. In practice, however, UK vendors of these goods also send a fax of their applications to the Communications and Electronics Security Group (CESG), simultaneously with the transmittal of the application to DTI so as to speed up the decision process. CESG is part of GCHQ, the UK's NSA equivalent, but has a separate identity to facilitate work with unclassified commercial entities. CESG reviews the application and (on paper) advises DTI of its view. In practice, DTI generally follows the CESG recommendation and does not approve the export item that CESG finds unacceptable."

On January 28, 1998, the DTI authorized an "Open General Export License" for personal computers accompanying their users that contain encryption. On-line voice encryption/decryption programs are not covered by the special permit.

Ref: Inventory of Controls on Cryptography Technologies, Group of Experts on Information Security and Privacy, Organization for Economic Cooperation and Development (DSTI/ICCP/REG(98)4/REV3), 23 September 1998.

Cyber-Rights & Cyber-Liberties (UK) Response to the Secure Electronic Commerce Statement, April 28, 1998 <http://www.cyber-rights.org/crypto/ecsresp.htm>

Department of Trade and Industry, "Proposals For Secure Electronic Commerce Bill Published," PN/98/320, 27 April, 1998 <http://www.coi.gov.uk/coi/depts/GTI/coi0803e.ok>

Department of Trade and Industry, Secure Electronic Commerce Statement is available at <http://www.dti.gov.uk/CII/ana27p.html>

Global Internet Liberty Campaign Member Statement: New UK Encryption Policy criticised, February 1998, is available at http://www.leeds.ac.uk/law/pgs/yaman/crypto-uk.html.

A Study of the International Market for Computer Software with Encryption , U.S. Department of Commerce and the National Security Agency, July 1995.

United States

1999 YELLOW

1998 YELLOW/RED

There are no domestic use or import controls on cryptography in the United States.

The Federal Bureau of Investigation has several times proposed legislation that would require all manufacturers of encryption products and network services to include key recovery or escrow mechanisms to enable "immediate decryption of communications or electronic information encrypted by such products or services on the public network." The FBI proposal would also empower the Attorney General to act as final arbiter of whether an encryption method conforms to government eavesdropping standards. No new technology with encryption mechanisms would be able to be manufactured, sold, resold, distributed or imported without the prior approval of the chief law enforcement official of the United States.

The FBI, assisted by the NSA, Justice Department and Defense Department, has actively lobbied domestic and international organizations for encryption access programs. These include the federal legislative and judicial branches, business organizations, law enforcement associations, religious groups, as well as international organizations, such as the Group of 8 (G8), the OECD, the European Union, the Council of Europe, the Asia-Pacific Economic Council (APEC), the Association of South-East Asian Nations (ASEAN), NATO, International Standards Organization (ISO), the Wassenaar Arrangement participants, and the Financial Action Task Force (FATF).

The United States, as the primary force behind the Wassenaar Arrangement and its predecessor COCOM, maintains export controls on cryptographic hardware and software products. The United States was a primary architect of the changes to the Wassenaar Dual-Use Control List announced in December 1998, although it did not succeed in advancing the concept of key recovery and extension of the dual-use list to cover intangible exports of cryptography. The export of non-military cryptographic hardware and software is administered by the Bureau of Export Administration (BXA), a component of the Department of Commerce.

In 1996, the International Traffic in Arms Regulation governing the export of cryptography was overhauled. Responsibility for cryptography exports was transferred to the Department of Commerce from the Department of State.

However, the Department of Justice is now part of the export review process. In addition, the National Security Agency (NSA) remains the final arbiter of whether to grant encryption products export licenses. NSA staff are assigned to the Commerce Department and several other federal agencies that deal with encryption policy and standards, including the State Department, Justice Department, National Institute for Standards and Technology (NIST), and the Federal Communications Commission.

On September 16, 1998 the government announced plans for revised export control requirements. On December 31, 1998, the BXA announced the new licensing requirements for cryptographic exports:

> The key recovery agent requirements for license exception Key Management Infrastructure (KMI) eligibility for exports and re-exports of recovery encryption commodities and software were eliminated. Also eliminated were key recovery commitment plans and the six-month progress reviews previously required. Exporters are no longer required to name or submit to BXA additional information on a key recovery agent prior to export.
>
> License exceptions were authorized for financial-specific encryption commodities and software and general purpose encryption commodities and software for banks and financial institutions.
>
> Exports and re-exports of encryption commodities, software and technology, including source code of any key length, are also eligible under a license exception to U.S. subsidiaries for internal company proprietary use to all destinations except Cuba, Iran, Iraq, Libya, North Korea, Sudan and Syria. Encryption chips, integrated circuits, toolkits, executable or linkable modules which can modify or enhance the cryptographic functionality (e.g., the confidentiality algorithm, key space and key exchange mechanism) or incorporate the cryptographic function in another item, are eligible for license exception only for export to U.S. subsidiaries.
>
> Exports to "strategic partners" of U.S. companies, such as subcontractors and joint ventures, will be considered favorably under a license when the end-use is for the protection of U.S. company proprietary information.

Encryption commodities, including mass market and non-mass market software incorporating symmetric algorithms with key lengths up to and including 56-bits, such as DES or equivalent (such as RC2, RC4, RC5 and CAST) are authorized for license exception to all destinations except Cuba, Iran, Iraq, Libya, North Korea, Sudan and Syria. Encryption chips, integrated circuits, toolkits and executable or linkable modules are not authorized for export under License Exception and require a license or an Encryption Licensing Arrangement. Subsequent bundling, updates or releases may be exported and re-exported under applicable provisions of the EAR without a separate technical review as long as the functional encryption capacity of the originally reviewed encryption commodities, including mass market and non-mass market, and non-mass market software has not been modified or enhanced.

Encryption commodities and software of any key length are authorized to insurance companies, health and medical end-users in 45 countries. Exports and re-exports of such commodities and software are not eligible under License Exception to non-U.S. biochemical and pharmaceutical manufacturers and non-U.S. military health and medical entities.

Encryption commodities and software of any key length are authorized for on-line merchants in 45 countries. Such commodities and software must be limited to client-server applications (e.g., Secure Socket Layer (SSL) based applications) or applications specially designed for on-line transactions. End-use is limited to the purchase or sale of goods and software; and services connected with the purchase or sale of goods and software, including interactions between purchasers and sellers necessary for ordering, payment and delivery of goods and software. No other end-uses or customer to customer communications or transactions are allowed. Foreign on-line merchants or their separate business units who are engaged in the manufacturing and distribution of items or services controlled on the U.S. Munitions List (e.g., arms manufacturers) are excluded. Foreign government end-users also are excluded from this License Exception. It does not include such end-uses as general purpose messaging, collaborative research projects (e.g., collaborative engineering), data

> warehousing, remote computing services or electronic communications services.

There are several inconsistencies associated with the revised export control regulations. License exceptions are granted to 28 Tier 1 countries. Tier 1 countries are Western Europe, Japan, Canada, Mexico, Australia, and New Zealand. However, Mexico is not one of the 45 countries granted license exception relief. Also, four Tier 1 countries having free trade agreements with countries granted license exceptions are not included on the list: Andorra, Liechtenstein, San Marino, and the Vatican City State.

License exceptions are granted to 17 Tier 2 countries. Tier 2 countries include Latin America, South Korea, the Association of Southeast Asian Nations, Hungary, Poland, Czech Republic, Slovak Republic, Slovenia, and South Africa. Eleven of the 17 have no special relationship with the United States, such as participation in Wassenaar.

Only one Tier 3 country, Croatia, was included on the list. Tier 3 countries include 50 countries (India, Pakistan, all Middle East/Maghreb, the former Soviet Union, China, Vietnam, rest of Eastern Europe). Four Tier 3 countries having a special relationship with the United States through Wassenaar are not eligible for export licensing relief. They are Bulgaria, Romania, Russia, and Ukraine.

Stringent export controls continue to apply to seven Tier 4 countries subject to an embargo. They are Iraq, Iran, Libya, North Korea, Cuba, Sudan, and Syria.

The inconsistencies appear to be a result of problems associated with agreeing to mutual access to cryptographic information through Mutual Legal Assistance Treaties (MLATs) and other law enforcement information sharing agreements.

In May 1999, a federal appeals court affirmed the judgment of a lower court and held that the Export Administration Regulations unconstitutionally limit the freedom to distribute encryption software. The court said:

> The government defendants appeal the grant of summary judgment to the plaintiff, Professor Daniel J. Bernstein ("Bernstein"), enjoining the enforcement of certain Export

> Administration Regulations ("EAR") that limit Bernstein's ability to distribute encryption software. We find that the EAR regulations (1) operate as a prepublication licensing scheme that burdens scientific expression, (2) vest boundless discretion in government officials, and (3) lack adequate procedural safeguards. Consequently, we hold that the challenged regulations constitute a prior restraint on speech that offends the First Amendment. Although we employ a somewhat narrower rationale than did the district court, its judgment is accordingly affirmed.

Ref: http://www.epic.org/crypto/export_controls/bxa-regs-1298.html
Inventory of Controls on Cryptography Technologies, Group of Experts on Information Security and Privacy, Organization for Economic Cooperation and Development (DSTI/ICCP/REG(98)4/REV3), 23 September 1998.
White House Press Announcement, September 16, 1998.
Bernstein v. Department of Justice (CA9 1999)
http://www.epic.org/crypto/export_controls/bernstein_decision_9_cir.html

Uruguay

1999 GREEN/YELLOW
1998 Not reported

There are reportedly no export, import, or domestic use controls on cryptography in Uruguay.

On September 16, 1998, the United States authorized the export of unlimited strength encryption products (with or without key recovery) to the banking and financial, insurance, health and medical, and on-line electronic commercial sectors in Uruguay. This is an indication that the U.S. has leveraged its authority to gain access to plain text information in those sectors within the country under Mutual Legal Assistance Treaty (MLAT)/Financial Action Task Force (FATF) provisions.

Ref: White House Press Announcement, September 16, 1998

Venezuela

1999 RED
1998 Not reported

Venezuela officially prohibits both the import and domestic use of encryption products and software for non-government use. The Judicial Technical Police, the chief criminal intelligence agency in the country, monitors networks for encryption use.

Vietnam

1999 RED
1998 Not reported

Vietnam strictly controls the import, export, and domestic use of cryptographic products. In 1998, the Prime Minister received a report from the Government Cryptography Committee on a draft ordinance on cryptography. The government reviewed the draft ordinance, with particular regard to the scope and title of the ordinance.

The government authorized the Government Cryptography Committee to coordinate its activities with other relevant departments to finalize the draft ordinance and submit it to the Prime Minister for presentation to the Political Bureau of the Communist Party for its endorsement.

Ref: Voice of Vietnam, Hanoi, in Vietnamese 1430 GMT, October 30, 1998, BBC Summary of World Broadcasts, November 9, 1998.

Table of Countries

Green	Green/Yellow	Yellow	Yellow/Red	Red	Unknown
Anguilla Antigua and Barbuda Aruba Belize Campione d'Italia *Canada* Chile Crotia *Cyprus* Dominica Estonia Falkland Islands Germany Gibralter Iceland *Indonesia* *Ireland* Kuwait *Krgystan* Latvia Lebanon Liechtenstein Lithuania Mexico Monaco Morocco Mount Athos Naru Niue Norfolk Island Papua New Guinea Philippines Pitcairn Islands Slovenia Sri Lanka Swaziland Switzerland Tanzania Tonga Uganda United Arab Emirates	*Argentina* *Armenia* Australia *Austria* **Belgium** **Brazil** Bulgaria Czech Republic **Denmark** **Finland** *France* Greece Hungary Italy *Japan* Kenya *South Korea* Luxembourg Netherlands Netherlands Antilles New Zealand **Norway** Poland Portugal Romania *South Africa* **Sweden** *Taiwan* *Turkey* *Ukraine* Uruguay	Hong Kong Malaysia **Slovakia** Spain **United Kingdom** *United States*	India Israel **Saudi Arabia**	Belarus China Kazakhstan Pakistan Russia Singapore Tunisia Venezuala Vietnam	Angola Bahrain Cambodia Iran Mongolia Myanmar Nicaragua Palestine Tatarstan

Key:

Bold indicates that the country adopted a more restrictive policy.

Italics indicate that the country adopted a less restrictive policy.

Normal indicates that the country's policy remained largely unchanged.

OECD Guidelines

Organisation for Economic Cooperation and Development

RECOMMENDATION OF THE COUNCIL

CONCERNING GUIDELINES FOR CRYPTOGRAPHY POLICY

27 March 1997

THE COUNCIL,

HAVING REGARD TO:

- the Convention on the Organisation for Economic Co-operation and Development of 14 December 1960, in particular, articles 1 (b), 1 (c), 3 (a) and 5 (b) thereof;

- the Recommendation of the Council concerning Guidelines Governing the Protection of Privacy and Transborder Flows of Personal Data of 23 September 1980 [C(80)58/FINAL];

- the Declaration on Transborder Data Flows adopted by the Governments of OECD Member countries on 11 April 1985 [Annex to C(85)139];

- the Recommendation of the Council concerning Guidelines for the Security of Information Systems of 26-27 November 1992 [C(92)188/FINAL];

- the Directive [95/46/EC] of the European Parliament and of the Council of the European Union of 24 October 1995 on the protection of individuals with regard to the processing of personal data and on the free movement of such data;

- the Wassenaar Arrangement on Export Controls for Conventional Arms and Dual-use Goods and Technologies agreed on 13 July 1996;

• the Decision [94/942/PESC] and Regulation [(CE) 3381/94] of the Council of the European Union of July 1995 on the export of dual-use goods;

• and the Recommendation [R(95)13] of the Council of Europe of 11 September 1995 concerning problems of criminal procedural law connected with information technology;

CONSIDERING:

• that national and global information infrastructures are developing rapidly to provide a seamless network for world-wide communications and access to data;

• that this emerging information and communications network is likely to have an important impact on economic development and world trade;

• that the users of information technology must have trust in the security of information and communications infrastructures, networks and systems; in the confidentiality, integrity, and availability of data on them; and in the ability to prove the origin and receipt of data;

• that data is increasingly vulnerable to sophisticated threats to its security, and ensuring the security of data through legal, procedural and technical means is fundamentally important in order for national and international information infrastructures to reach their full potential;

RECOGNISING:

• that, as cryptography can be an effective tool for the secure use of information technology by ensuring confidentiality, integrity and availability of data and by providing authentication and non-repudiation mechanisms for that data, it is an important component of secure information and communications networks and systems;

• that cryptography has a variety of applications related to the protection of privacy, intellectual property, business and financial information, public safety and national security, and the operation of electronic commerce, including secure anonymous payments and transactions;

• that the failure to utilise cryptographic methods can adversely affect the protection of privacy, intellectual property, business and financial information, public safety and national security and the operation of electronic commerce because data and communications may be inadequately protected from unauthorised access, alteration, and improper use, and, therefore, users may not trust information and communications systems, networks and infrastructures;

• that the use of cryptography to ensure integrity of data, including authentication and non-repudiation mechanisms, is distinct from its use to ensure confidentiality of data, and that each of these uses presents different issues;

• that the quality of information protection afforded by cryptography depends not only on the selected technical means, but also on good managerial, organisational and operational procedures;

AND FURTHER RECOGNISING:

• that governments have wide-ranging responsibilities, several of which are specifically implicated in the use of cryptography, including protection of privacy and facilitating information and communications systems security; encouraging economic well-being by, in part, promoting commerce; maintaining public safety; and enabling the enforcement of laws and the protection of national security;

• that although there are legitimate governmental, commercial and individual needs and uses for cryptography, it may also be used by individuals or entities for illegal activities, which can affect public safety, national security, the enforcement of laws, business interests, consumer interests or privacy; therefore governments, together with industry and the general public, are challenged to develop balanced policies;

• that due to the inherently global nature of information and communications networks, implementation of incompatible national policies will not meet the needs of individuals, business and governments and may create obstacles to economic co-operation and development; and, therefore, national policies may require international co-ordination;

• that this Recommendation of the Council does not affect the sovereign rights of national governments and that the Guidelines contained in the Annex to this Recommendation are always subject to the requirements of national law;

On the proposal of the Committee for Information, Computer and Communications Policy;

RECOMMENDS THAT MEMBER COUNTRIES:

• establish new, or amend existing, policies, methods, measures, practices and procedures to reflect and take into account the Principles concerning cryptography policy set forth in the Guidelines contained in the Annex to this Recommendation (hereinafter "the Guidelines"), which is an integral part hereof; in so doing, also take into account the Recommendation of the Council concerning Guidelines Governing the Protection of Privacy and Transborder Flows of Personal Data of 23 September 1980 [C(80)58/FINAL] and the Recommendation of the Council concerning Guidelines for the Security of Information Systems of 26-27 November 1992 [C(92)188/FINAL];

• consult, co-ordinate and co-operate at the national and international level in the implementation of the Guidelines;

• act on the need for practical and operational solutions in the area of international cryptography policy by using the Guidelines as a basis for agreements on specific issues related to international cryptography policy;

• disseminate the Guidelines throughout the public and private sectors to promote awareness of the issues and policies related to cryptography;

• remove, or avoid creating in the name of cryptography policy, unjustified obstacles to international trade and the development of information and communications networks;

• state clearly and make publicly available, any national controls imposed by governments relating to the use of cryptography;

• review the Guidelines at least every five years, with a view to improving international co-operation on issues relating to cryptography policy.

ANNEX

GUIDELINES FOR CRYPTOGRAPHY POLICY

I. AIMS

The Guidelines are intended:

• to promote the use of cryptography:

• to foster confidence in information and communications infrastructures, networks and systems and the manner in which they are used;

• to help ensure the security of data, and to protect privacy, in national and global information and communications infrastructures, networks and systems;

• to promote this use of cryptography without unduly jeopardising public safety, law enforcement, and national security;

• to raise awareness of the need for compatible cryptography policies and laws, as well as the need for interoperable, portable and mobile cryptographic methods in national and global information and communications networks;

• to assist decision-makers in the public and private sectors in developing and implementing coherent national and international policies, methods, measures, practices and procedures for the effective use of cryptography;

• to promote co-operation between the public and private sectors in the development and implementation of national and international cryptography policies, methods, measures, practices and procedures;

• to facilitate international trade by promoting cost-effective, interoperable, portable and mobile cryptographic systems;

• to promote international co-operation among governments, business and research communities, and standards-making bodies in achieving co-ordinated use of cryptographic methods.

II. SCOPE

The Guidelines are primarily aimed at governments, in terms of the policy recommendations herein, but with anticipation that they will be widely read and followed by both the private and public sectors.

It is recognised that governments have separable and distinct responsibilities for the protection of information which requires security in the national interest; the Guidelines are not intended for application in these matters.

III. DEFINITIONS

For the purposes of the Guidelines:

• "Authentication" means a function for establishing the validity of a claimed identity of a user, device or another entity in an information or communications system.

• "Availability" means the property that data, information, and information and communications systems are accessible and usable on a timely basis in the required manner.

• "Confidentiality" means the property that data or information is not made available or disclosed to unauthorised individuals, entities, or processes.

• "Cryptography" means the discipline which embodies principles, means, and methods for the transformation of data in order to hide its information content, establish its authenticity, prevent its undetected modification, prevent its repudiation, and/or prevent its unauthorised use.

• "Cryptographic key" means a parameter used with a cryptographic algorithm to transform, validate, authenticate, encrypt or decrypt data.

• "Cryptographic methods" means cryptographic techniques, services, systems, products and key management systems.

• "Data" means the representation of information in a manner suitable for communication, interpretation, storage, or processing.

• "Decryption" means the inverse function of encryption.

• "Encryption" means the transformation of data by the use of cryptography to produce unintelligible data (encrypted data) to ensure its confidentiality.

• "Integrity" means the property that data or information has not been modified or altered in an unauthorised manner.

• "Interoperability" of cryptographic methods means the technical ability of multiple cryptographic methods to function together.

• "Key management system" means a system for generation, storage, distribution, revocation, deletion, archiving, certification or application of cryptographic keys.

• "Keyholder" means an individual or entity in possession or control of cryptographic keys. A keyholder is not necessarily a user of the key.

• "Law enforcement" or "enforcement of laws" refers to the enforcement of all laws, without regard to subject matter.

• "Lawful access" means access by third party individuals or entities, including governments, to plaintext, or cryptographic keys, of encrypted data, in accordance with law.

• "Mobility" of cryptographic methods only means the technical ability to function in multiple countries or information and communications infrastructures.

• "Non-repudiation" means a property achieved through cryptographic methods, which prevents an individual or entity from denying having performed a particular action related to data (such as mechanisms for non-rejection of authority (origin); for proof of obligation, intent, or commitment; or for proof of ownership).

• "Personal data" means any information relating to an identified or identifiable individual.

• "Plaintext" means intelligible data.

• "Portability" of cryptographic methods means the technical ability to be adapted and function in multiple systems.

IV. INTEGRATION

The principles in Section V of this Annex, each of which addresses an important policy concern, are interdependent and should be implemented as a whole so as to balance the various interests at stake. No principle should be implemented in isolation from the rest.

V. PRINCIPLES

1. TRUST IN CRYPTOGRAPHIC METHODS

CRYPTOGRAPHIC METHODS SHOULD BE TRUSTWORTHY IN ORDER TO GENERATE CONFIDENCE IN THE USE OF INFORMATION AND COMMUNICATIONS SYSTEMS.

Market forces should serve to build trust in reliable systems, and government regulation, licensing, and use of cryptographic methods may also encourage user trust. Evaluation of cryptographic methods, especially against market-accepted criteria, could also generate user trust.

In the interests of user trust, a contract dealing with the use of a key management system should indicate the jurisdiction whose laws apply to that system.

2. CHOICE OF CRYPTOGRAPHIC METHODS

USERS SHOULD HAVE A RIGHT TO CHOOSE ANY CRYPTOGRAPHIC METHOD, SUBJECT TO APPLICABLE LAW.

Users should have access to cryptography that meets their needs, so that they can trust in the security of information and communications systems, and the confidentiality and integrity of data on those systems. Individuals or entities who own, control, access, use or store data may have a responsibility to protect the confidentiality and integrity of such data, and may therefore be responsible for using appropriate cryptographic methods. It is expected that a variety of cryptographic methods may be needed to fulfil different data security requirements. Users of cryptography should be free, subject to applicable law, to determine the type and level of data security needed, and to select and implement appropriate cryptographic methods, including a key management system that suits their needs.

In order to protect an identified public interest, such as the protection of personal data or electronic commerce, governments may implement policies requiring cryptographic methods to achieve a sufficient level of protection.

Government controls on cryptographic methods should be no more than are essential to the discharge of government responsibilities and should respect user choice to the greatest extent possible. This principle should not be interpreted as implying that governments should initiate legislation which limits user choice.

3. MARKET DRIVEN DEVELOPMENT OF CRYPTOGRAPHIC METHODS

CRYPTOGRAPHIC METHODS SHOULD BE DEVELOPED IN RESPONSE TO THE NEEDS, DEMANDS AND RESPONSIBILITIES OF INDIVIDUALS, BUSINESSES AND GOVERNMENTS.

The development and provision of cryptographic methods should be determined by the market in an open and competitive environment. Such an approach would best ensure that solutions keep pace with changing technology, the demands of users and evolving threats to information and communications systems security. The development of international technical standards, criteria and protocols related to cryptographic methods should also be market driven. Governments should encourage and co-operate with business and the research community in the development of cryptographic methods.

4. STANDARDS FOR CRYPTOGRAPHIC METHODS

TECHNICAL STANDARDS, CRITERIA AND PROTOCOLS FOR CRYPTOGRAPHIC METHODS SHOULD BE DEVELOPED AND PROMULGATED AT THE NATIONAL AND INTERNATIONAL LEVEL.

In response to the needs of the market, internationally-recognised standards-making bodies, governments, business and other relevant experts should share information and collaborate to develop and promulgate interoperable technical standards, criteria and protocols for cryptographic methods. National standards for cryptographic methods, if any, should be consistent with international standards to facilitate global interoperability, portability and mobility. Mechanisms to evaluate conformity to such technical standards, criteria and protocols for interoperability, portability and mobility of cryptographic methods should be developed. To the extent that testing of conformity to, or evaluation of, standards may occur, the broad acceptance of such results should be encouraged.

5. PROTECTION OF PRIVACY AND PERSONAL DATA

THE FUNDAMENTAL RIGHTS OF INDIVIDUALS TO PRIVACY, INCLUDING SECRECY OF COMMUNICATIONS AND PROTECTION OF PERSONAL DATA, SHOULD BE RESPECTED IN NATIONAL CRYPTOGRAPHY POLICIES AND IN THE IMPLEMENTATION AND USE OF CRYPTOGRAPHIC METHODS.

Cryptographic methods can be a valuable tool for the protection of privacy, including both the confidentiality of data and communications and the protection of the identity of individuals. Cryptographic methods also offer new opportunities to minimise the collection of personal data, by enabling secure but anonymous payments, transactions and interactions. At the same time, cryptographic methods to ensure the integrity of data in electronic transactions raise privacy implications. These implications, which include the collection of personal data and the creation of systems for personal identification, should be considered and explained, and, where appropriate, privacy safeguards should be established.

The OECD Guidelines for the Protection of Privacy and Transborder Flows of Personal Data provide general guidance concerning the collection and management of personal information, and should be applied in concert with relevant national law when implementing cryptographic methods.

6. LAWFUL ACCESS

NATIONAL CRYPTOGRAPHY POLICIES MAY ALLOW LAWFUL ACCESS TO PLAINTEXT, OR CRYPTOGRAPHIC KEYS, OF ENCRYPTED DATA. THESE POLICIES MUST RESPECT THE OTHER PRINCIPLES CONTAINED IN THE GUIDELINES TO THE GREATEST EXTENT POSSIBLE.

If considering policies on cryptographic methods that provide for lawful access, governments should carefully weigh the benefits, including the benefits for public safety, law enforcement and national security, as well as the risks of misuse, the additional expense of any supporting infrastructure, the prospects of technical failure, and other costs. This principle should not be interpreted as implying that governments should, or should not, initiate legislation that would allow lawful access.

Where access to the plaintext, or cryptographic keys, of encrypted data is requested under lawful process, the individual or entity requesting access must have a legal right to possession of the plaintext, and once obtained the data must only be used for lawful purposes. The process through which lawful access is obtained should be recorded, so that the disclosure of the cryptographic keys or the data can be audited or reviewed in accordance with national law. Where lawful access is requested and obtained, such access should be granted within designated time limits appropriate to the circumstances. The conditions of lawful access should be stated clearly and published in a way that they are easily available to users, keyholders and providers of cryptographic methods.

Key management systems could provide a basis for a possible solution which could balance the interest of users and law enforcement authorities; these techniques could also be used to recover data, when keys are lost. Processes for lawful access to cryptographic keys must recognise the distinction between keys which are used to protect confidentiality and keys which are used for other purposes only. A cryptographic key that provides for identity or integrity only (as distinct from a cryptographic key that verifies identity or integrity only) should not be made available without the consent of the individual or entity in lawful possession of that key.

7. LIABILITY

WHETHER ESTABLISHED BY CONTRACT OR LEGISLATION, THE LIABILITY OF INDIVIDUALS AND ENTITIES THAT OFFER CRYPTOGRAPHIC SERVICES OR HOLD OR ACCESS CRYPTOGRAPHIC KEYS SHOULD BE CLEARLY STATED.

The liability of any individual or entity, including a government entity, that offers cryptographic services or holds or has access to cryptographic keys, should be made clear by contract or where appropriate by national legislation or international agreement. The liability of users for misuse of their own keys should also be made clear. A keyholder should not be held liable for providing cryptographic keys or plaintext of encrypted data in accordance with lawful access. The party that obtains lawful access should be liable for misuse of cryptographic keys or plaintext that it has obtained.

8. INTERNATIONAL CO-OPERATION

GOVERNMENTS SHOULD CO-OPERATE TO CO-ORDINATE CRYPTOGRAPHY POLICIES. AS PART OF THIS EFFORT, GOVERNMENTS SHOULD REMOVE, OR AVOID CREATING IN THE NAME OF CRYPTOGRAPHY POLICY, UNJUSTIFIED OBSTACLES TO TRADE.

In order to promote the broad international acceptance of cryptography and enable the full potential of the national and global information and communications networks, cryptography policies adopted by a country should be co-ordinated as much as possible with similar policies of other countries. To that end, the Guidelines should be used for national policy formulation.

If developed, national key management systems must, where appropriate, allow for international use of cryptography.

Lawful access across national borders may be achieved through bilateral and multilateral co-operation and agreement.

No government should impede the free flow of encrypted data passing through its jurisdiction merely on the basis of cryptography policy.

In order to promote international trade, governments should avoid developing cryptography policies and practices which create unjustified obstacles to global electronic commerce. Governments should avoid creating unjustified obstacles to international availability of cryptographic methods.

Wassenaar Arrangement

<u>WA LIST (98) 1</u>
03-12-98

THE WASSENAAR ARRANGEMENT

ON

EXPORT CONTROLS FOR CONVENTIONAL ARMS AND DUAL-USE GOODS AND TECHNOLOGIES

LIST OF DUAL-USE GOODS AND TECHNOLOGIES **AND** MUNITIONS LIST

<u>Category 5, Part 2 - "INFORMATION SECURITY"</u>

<u>Note 1</u> *The control status of "information security" equipment, "software", systems, application specific "electronic assemblies", modules, integrated circuits, components or functions is determined in Category 5, Part 2 even if they are components or "electronic assemblies" of other equipment.*

<u>Note 2</u> *Category 5 Part 2 does not control products when accompanying their user for the user's personal use.*

<u>Note 3</u> *<u>Cryptography Note</u>*

5.A.2. and 5.D.2. do not control items that meet all of the following:

a. Generally available to the public by being sold, without restriction, from stock at retail selling points by means of any of the following:
  1. Over-the-counter transactions;
  2. Mail order transactions;
  3. Electronic transactions; <u>or</u>
  4. Telephone call transactions;

b. The cryptographic functionality cannot easily be changed by the user;

c. *Designed for installation by the user without further substantial support by the supplier;*
d. *Does not contain a "symmetric algorithm" employing a key length exceeding 64 bits; and*
e. *When necessary, details of the items are accessible and will be provided, upon request, to the appropriate authority in the exporter's country in order to ascertain compliance with conditions described in paragraphs a. to d. above.*

Technical Note
In Category 5 - Part 2, parity bits are not included in the key length.

5. A. 2. SYSTEMS, EQUIPMENT AND COMPONENTS

a. Systems, equipment, application specific "electronic assemblies", modules and integrated circuits for "information security", as follows, and other specially designed components therefor:

N.B. *For the control of global navigation satellite systems receiving equipment containing or employing decryption (i.e. GPS or GLONASS), see 7.A.5.*

5. A. 2. a. 1. Designed or modified to use "cryptography" employing digital techniques performing any cryptographic function other than authentication or digital signature having any of the following:
Technical Notes
1. *Authentication and digital signature functions include their associated key management function.*
2. *Authentication includes all aspects of access control where there is no encryption of files or text except as directly related to the protection of passwords, Personal Identification Numbers (PINs) or similar data to prevent unauthorised access.*
3. *"Cryptography" does not include "fixed" data compression or coding techniques.*

Note *5.A.2.a.1. includes equipment designed or modified to use "cryptography" employing analogue principles when implemented with digital techniques.*

5. A. 2. a. 1. a. A "symmetric algorithm" employing a key length in excess of 56 bits; <u>or</u>

b. An "asymmetric algorithm" where the security of the algorithm is based on any of the following:

1. Factorisation of integers in excess of 512 bits (e.g., RSA);
2. Computation of discrete logarithms in a multiplicative group of a finite field of size greater than 512 bits (e.g., Diffie-Hellman over Z/pZ); <u>or</u>
3. Discrete logarithms in a group other than mentioned in 5.A.2.a.1.b.2. in excess of 112 bits (e.g., Diffie-Hellman over an elliptic curve);

2. Designed or modified to perform cryptanalytic functions;

3. Deleted;

4. Specially designed or modified to reduce the compromising emanations of information-bearing signals beyond what is necessary for health, safety or electromagnetic interference standards;

5. Designed or modified to use cryptographic techniques to generate the spreading code for "spread spectrum" or the hopping code for "frequency agility" systems;

6. Designed or modified to provide certified or certifiable "multilevel security" or user isolation at a level exceeding Class B2 of the Trusted Computer System Evaluation Criteria (TCSEC) or equivalent;

7. Communications cable systems designed or modified using mechanical, electrical or electronic means to detect surreptitious intrusion.

<u>*Note*</u> *5.A.2. does not control:*

a. "Personalised smart cards" where the cryptographic capability is restricted for use in equipment or systems excluded from control under entries b. to f. of this Note;

N.B. If a "personalised smart card" has multiple functions, the control status of each function is assessed individually.

b. Receiving equipment for radio broadcast, pay television or similar restricted audience television of the consumer type, without digital encryption except that exclusively used for sending the billing or programme-related information back to the broadcast providers;

c. Equipment where the cryptographic capability is not user-accessible and which is specially designed and limited to allow any of the following:
   1. Execution of copy-protected software;
   2. Access to any of the following:
      a. Copy-protected read-only media; or
      b. Information stored in encrypted form on media (e.g. in connection with the protection of intellectual property rights) when the media is offered for sale in identical sets to the public; or
   3. One-time copying of copyright protected audio/video data.

d. Cryptographic equipment specially designed and limited for banking use or money transactions;
Technical Note
'Money transactions' in 5.A.2. Note d. includes the collection and settlement of fares or credit functions.

e. Portable or mobile radiotelephones for civil use (e.g., for use with commercial civil cellular radiocommunications systems) that are not capable of end-to-end encryption;

f. Cordless telephone equipment not capable of end-to-end encryption where the maximum effective range of unboosted cordless operation (i.e., a single, unrelayed hop between terminal and home basestation) is less than 400 metres according to the manufacturer's specifications.

5. B. 2. TEST, INSPECTION AND PRODUCTION EQUIPMENT

a. Equipment specially designed for:

   1. The "development" of equipment or functions controlled by Category 5 - Part 2, including measuring or test equipment;
   2. The "production" of equipment or functions controlled by Category 5 - Part 2, including measuring, test, repair or production equipment.

b. Measuring equipment specially designed to evaluate and validate the "information security" functions controlled by 5.A.2. or 5.D.2.

5. C. 2. MATERIALS - None

5. D. 2. SOFTWARE

a. "Software" specially designed or modified for the "development", "production" or "use" of equipment or "software" controlled by Category 5 - Part 2;
b. "Software" specially designed or modified to support "technology" controlled by 5.E.2.;
c. Specific "software", as follows:
   1. "Software" having the characteristics, or performing or simulating the functions of the equipment controlled by 5.A.2. or 5.B.2.;
   2. "Software" to certify "software" controlled by 5.D.2.c.1.

Note *5.D.2. does not control:*
a. "Software" required for the "use" of equipment excluded from control under the Note to 5.A.2.;
b. "Software" providing any of the functions of equipment excluded from control under the Note to 5.A.2.

5. E. 2. TECHNOLOGY

a. "Technology" according to the General Technology Note for the "development", "production" or "use" of equipment or "software" controlled by Category 5 - Part 2.

GILC Resolution on Cryptography

RESOLUTION IN SUPPORT OF THE FREEDOM TO USE CRYPTOGRAPHY

25 SEPTEMBER 1996
PARIS, FRANCE

WHEREAS the Organization for Economic Cooperation and Development (OECD) is now considering the development of an international policy for the use of cryptography;

WHEREAS the use of cryptography implicates human rights and matters of personal liberty that affect individuals around the world;

WHEREAS national governments have already taken steps to detain and to harass users and developers of cryptography technology;

WHEREAS cryptography is already in use by human rights advocates who face persecution by their national governments;

WHEREAS the privacy of communication is explicitly protected by Article 12 of the Universal Declaration of Human Rights, Article 17 of the International Covenant on Civil and Political Rights, and national law;

WHEREAS cryptography will play an increasingly important role in the ability of citizens to protect their privacy in the Information Society;

RECOGNIZING that the OECD has made substantial contributions to the preservation of human rights and the protection of privacy;

FURTHER RECOGNIZING that decisions about cryptography policy may gives rise to communication networks that favor privacy or favor surveillance;

FURTHER RECOGNIZING that the promotion of key escrow encryption by government poses a direct threat to the privacy rights of citizens;

THE FOLLOWING NATIONAL AND INTERNATIONAL ORGANIZATIONS, concerned with matters of human rights, civil liberty, and personal freedom, have joined together to:

URGE the OECD to base its cryptography policies on the fundamental right of citizens to engage in private communication;

FURTHER URGE the OECD to resist policies that would encourage the development of communication networks designed for surveillance; and

RECOMMEND that the OECD turn its attention to growing public concerns about the widespread use of surveillance technologies and the implications for Democratic Society and Personal Liberty around the world.

RESPECTFULLY ENDORSED,

Associazione per la Libertà nella Comunicazione Elettronica Interattiva (ALCEI)
American Civil Liberties Union
Association des Utilisateurs d'Internet
CITADEL-EF France
Computer Professionals for Social Responsibility
cyberPOLIS
Digital Citizens Foundation in the Netherlands
EFF-Austin
Electronic Frontier Australia
Electronic Frontier Canada
Electronic Frontier Foundation
Electronic Privacy Information Center
Human Rights Watch
NetAction
Privacy International